Dis ord
sel (r)
1-27-10

MARYANN'S FAVORITE FAMILY RECIPES

ARU RICHARDSON

authorHOUSE®

AuthorHouse™
1663 Liberty Drive
Bloomington, IN 47403
www.authorhouse.com
Phone: 1-800-839-8640

First published by AuthorHouse 10/26/2009

ISBN: 978-1-4490-2403-1 (e)
ISBN: 978-1-4490-2401-7 (sc)
ISBN: 978-1-4490-2402-4 (hc)

Library of Congress Control Number: 2009911380

Printed in the United States of America
Bloomington, Indiana

This book is printed on acid-free paper.

LionWolf
http://www.lionwolfinc.com

Acknowledgements

To my grandma, who put her heart and soul into everything that she did in life. MaryAnn loved to cook for her family and friends. She kept many recipes over the years and wanted to write a cookbook. Therefore, I am honoring my grandma by completing her cookbook. I added some of my own recipes as well. My grandma was a wonderful woman that meant the world to me and taught me some of her cooking skills.

TABLE OF CONTENTS

BREADS

SALADS

SOUPS

DESSERTS

Breakfast

Vegetable Omelet

Ingredients:

   1 cup finely chopped broccoli
   ½ cup diced red bell pepper
   ½ cup shredded carrot
   ½ cup of cheddar cheese
   1/3 cup sliced green onions
   1 clove garlic, minced
   2 ½ Tbs olive oil
   1 tablespoon grated parmesan cheese
   ½ teaspoon Italian seasoning
   1 ½ cup eggs
   1/3 cup chopped tomato
   Chopped fresh parsley, for garnish

Directions: In a skillet, over medium-high heat sauté broccoli, bell pepper, carrot, green onions and garlic in 1 tablespoon of olive oil until softened. Remove from skillet, keep warm. Combine parmesan cheese, cheddar cheese and Italian seasoning; set aside. In same skillet, over medium heat, heat 1 ½-tablespoons of olive oil. Pour 1½-cups eggs into skillet. Cook, lifting edges to allow uncooked portion to flow underneath. When almost set, sprinkle the vegetable mixture on one half of the omelet and fold over other half to cover the vegetable mixture. Then slide omelet onto serving plate. Top omelet with tomato, and garnish with parsley.

BANANA-STUFFED FRENCH TOAST

INGREDIENTS:
  1 firm, ripe banana
  3/4 cup half-and-half
  2 large eggs
  1 teaspoon vanilla
  1/4 teaspoon cinnamon
  1/4 teaspoon freshly grated nutmeg
  4 (1-inch thick) slices wheat bread
  2 tablespoons unsalted butter
  Confectioners' sugar for dusting
  Warm maple syrup

DIRECTIONS: Cut banana into 1/4-inch thick slices. In a bowl, whisk together half-and-half, eggs, vanilla, cinnamon, and nutmeg. Make two sandwiches using the four slices of bread, each sandwich should have a layer of bananas. In a baking dish just large enough to hold bread slices in one layer, arrange bread slices and pour custard over them. Soak slices, turning them over once or twice to allow bread to absorb all liquid, about 15 minutes. In a 12-inch non-stick skillet melt butter over low heat until foam subsides and cook slices until golden, about 5 minutes on each side. Dust French toast with confectioners' sugar and serve with syrup.

Vegetable Quiche

INGREDIENTS:

- 4 eggs
- 1 ¼-cup milk
- 1-teaspoon salt
- ½-teaspoon pepper
- ¼ teaspoon garlic
- ¼ teaspoon parsley
- 1 cup of cheddar cheese
- 1 cup of Monterey Jack cheese
- 1 cup of Munster cheese
- 3 cups of sautéed hash browns
- 1 cup of onions
- 10oz. box of frozen mixed vegetables, thaw
- Pre-heated 350-degree oven

DIRECTIONS: Blend eggs, milk, and spices. Stir in cheese and mixed vegetables. Sauté 3 cups of hash browns and 1 cup of onion which will be used for the crust. Pour egg/cheese mixture into crust and bake for 35-40 minutes until firm in the center.

CRAB-AND-VEGETABLE QUICHE

INGREDIENTS:

Non-stick cooking spray
½ cup chopped yellow squash
½-cup broccoli chopped
2 tablespoons finely chopped onion
½ cup crabmeat
2 eggs
¼ cups milk
1/8 teaspoon cayenne pepper
1 tablespoon chopped fresh basil or ½ teaspoon dried basil

DIRECTIONS: Heat oven to 350 degrees. Spray 9 inch baking dish with cooking spray. Arrange vegetables and crabmeat in baking dish; sprinkle with cheese. In small mixing bowl, combine eggs, milk, pepper, and basil; pour over vegetables. Bake until filling is set, about 30 minutes.

THE PERFECT BISCUITS

INGREDIENTS:

    2 cups of self-rising flour
    2/3 cups of milk
    1/3 cup of vegetable or canola oil
    1 tablespoon of butter

DIRECTIONS: Mix quickly, the roll out and cut out 2-inch biscuits. Bake for 13 minutes at 450 degrees.

BREAKFAST BURRITOS WITH TOMATO-BASIL TOPPING

INGREDIENTS:

    2 large tomatoes, diced
    2 teaspoons finely chopped basil or ½ teaspoon dried basil leaves
    1 medium potato, peeled and shredded (about 1 cup)
    ¼ cup chopped onion
    2 teaspoons margarine
    1 cup eggs
    1/8 teaspoon ground black pepper
    4 (8 inch) flour tortillas, warmed
    1/3 cup shredded reduced-fat cheese

DIRECTIONS: In a small bowl, combine tomatoes and basil; set aside. In a large nonstick skillet, over medium heat, sauté potato and onion in spread until tender. Pour Egg Beaters into skillet; sprinkle with pepper. Cook, stirring occasionally, until mixture is set. Divide egg mixture evenly between tortillas; top with cheese. Fold tortillas over egg mixture. Top with tomato mixture.

Spinach and Mushrooms Enchiladas

Ingredients:
 2 packages (10 ounces each) frozen chopped spinach, thawed
 1 can (15 ounces) pinto beans, rinsed and drained, smashed
 1 can (15 ounces) black beans rinsed and drained, smashed
 1 can (15 ounces) kidney beans rinsed and drained, smashed
 1½ cup sliced mushrooms
 3 teaspoons chili powder, divided
 ¼-teaspoon red pepper flakes
 1 small onion, chopped
 1can (8 ounces) tomato sauce
 2 tablespoons of water
 ½-teaspoon hot pepper sauce
 8 (8-inch) corn tortillas
 1 cup (4 ounces) shredded Monterey Jack cheese
 Shredded lettuce
 Chopped tomatoes

Directions: Combine spinach, beans, mushrooms, 2 teaspoons chili powder, and red pepper in large skillet over medium heat. Cook and stir for 5 minutes; remove from heat. Combine tomato sauce, water, remaining 1-teaspoon chili powder and pepper sauce in medium skillet. Dip tortillas into tomato sauce mixture; stack tortillas on waxed paper. Divide spinach filling into 8 portions. Spoon onto centers of tortillas; roll up and place in microwaveable dish. Spread remaining tomato sauce mixture over enchiladas. Cover with vented plastic wrap. Microwave at medium (50% power) 10 minutes or until heat through. Sprinkle with cheese. Microwave at medium for 3 minutes or until cheese is melted. Serve with lettuce and tomatoes.

SPINACH QUICHE

INGREDIENTS:

½ cup chopped onion
1 clove garlic, crushed
1-teaspoon margarine or margarine substitute
1 (10-ounce) package frozen chopped spinach, thawed and well drained
1 (9-inch) pastry crust, unbaked
1 cup eggs
1 cup cheddar cheese
1 cup of Monterey Jack cheese
1 cup of Munster cheese
½ cup of milk

DIRECTIONS: Beat eggs, blend milk, spinach and spices into eggs. When mixed, stir in cheese. Pour in egg/cheese mixture and bake in pre-heated 350-degree oven for 35-40 minutes until firm in the center.

Drinks

Fruit Smoothies

INGREDIENTS:
- 1 ripe banana, sliced
- 4 strawberries,
- ½ cup of blueberries
- ¼ cup of mango, chopped
- ½ cup of cantaloupe, chopped
- ½ cup of honeydew melon, chopped
- ½ of kiwi
- ½ cup of watermelon, chopped
- 2 cups of orange juice

DIRECTIONS: Combine all ingredients in blender and blend on high until smooth. The frozen fruits will make the smoothies extra cold and frothy.

Pina Colada Smoothie

Ingredients:

    1 can (12 ounces) frozen pineapple juice concentrate, thawed

    1-pint low fat lime, orange, or lemon sherbet

    1 ¼ cup seltzer water

    ¾-teaspoon coconut extract

    Directions:

Combine all ingredients in blender and sherbet in small punch bowl or pitcher. Stir in seltzer water and coconut extract.

MANGO ICED TEA

INGREDIENTS:
- 1 ½ quarts cold water
- 6 high quality black tea bags
- 2 cups mango nectar
- Sugar
- thinly sliced mango

DIRECTIONS: Bring water to a boil, turn off heat add tea bags and steep until tea is dark, about 5 minutes. Remove bags, add mango nectar and add sugar, to taste. Stir until sugar is dissolved. Place in pitcher. Pour over ice and garnish with mango slices.

Hot Chocolate Drink

INGREDIENTS:

    3 cups milk

    ½ cup Dutch process unsweetened cocoa powder

    1 teaspoon vanilla extract

    ½ cup sugar

    1 tablespoon of instant coffee (regular or decaf.)

DIRECTIONS: In a saucepan, bring the milk to a low boil. Remove from the heat. Whisk the cocoa and vanilla into the milk. Add the sugar and simmer over medium heat, stirring, until the sugar is dissolved. Add the tablespoon of coffee and stir well. Remove from the heat and pour into mugs. Top with a spoonful of whipped cream.

Entrées

Coconut Curry Thai Chicken

INGREDIENTS:

Coconut Curry Sauce:
1 (13.5-ounce) can light coconut milk
1 tablespoon Thai curry paste
2 tablespoons curry powder
2 teaspoons minced fresh ginger
3 cloves garlic, minced
Dash cayenne pepper
Kosher salt and freshly ground black pepper
Chicken:
8 ounces high-fiber whole-wheat linguine
Olive oil cooking spray
1 Vidalia or other sweet onion, chopped
1 pound boneless skinless chicken breast, fat removed, cut into small pieces.
Kosher salt and freshly ground black pepper
2 tablespoons curry powder
2 tablespoons peanut butter
1 cup thinly sliced roasted red peppers
1 cup thinly sliced water chestnuts
1 cup scallions, white and green parts, thinly sliced
Chopped fresh mint and cilantro leaves, for garnish
Lime wedges, for serving

SAUCE: In a medium bowl, combine all of the sauce ingredients, whisk until thoroughly combined and set aside.

CHICKEN: Cook the whole-wheat linguine al dente according to box directions. Drain and rinse under cold water and spray lightly with olive oil cooking spray so it does not stick and set aside. Coat a large nonstick skillet with cooking spray and add onion. Cook until translucent and beginning to brown, about 5 to 10 minutes. Add the chicken, season with salt and pepper and stir in curry powder. Saute chicken until lightly brown. Add the peanut butter and allow it to melt to coat the chicken.

Add the roasted red peppers, water chestnuts and scallions and season with salt and pepper. Sauté for a few minutes just to release flavor. Pour the coconut milk sauce over the chicken and vegetables and stir gently. Cook just until warmed through and thickened a bit, about 3 to 5 minutes. Season with salt and pepper, as needed. Garnish with chopped mint and cilantro. Serve with lime wedges, if desired. Put linguine in a large deep bowl and pour mixture over the top. Toss gently with tongs. Garnish with fresh lime juice, and chopped scallions or herbs. You may substitute shrimp or tofu for the chicken.

GREEK SPINACH-CHEESE ROLLS

INGREDIENTS:

1 package of phyllo dough sheets
1 package (10 ounces) frozen chopped spinach, thawed and squeezed dry
¾ cup (3 ounces) crumbled feta cheese
½ cup (2 ounces) shredded reduced fat Monterey Jack Cheese
4 green onions, thinly sliced
1 teaspoon dried dill weed
½-teaspoon garlic powder
½-teaspoon black pepper

DIRECTIONS: Thaw phyllo sheets according to package directions. Combine spinach, cheeses, green onions, dill weed, garlic powder, and pepper in large bowl; mix well. Spoon spinach mixture evenly on 3 sheets of dough to within 1 inch of edges. Starting at long edge, roll snuggly using water along edge to seal. Place seam side down brush with oil, place on prepared oiled cookie sheet. Preheat oven to 375 degrees. Bake 20 to 25 minutes or until golden. Serve warm or at room temperature.

CHICKEN KIEV

INGREDIENTS:
- 4 whole large chicken breasts, halved lengthwise
- 2 tablespoons snipped parsley
- 1 tablespoon chopped green onion
- 1 ¼ pound stick of butter, well chilled
- 2 beaten eggs
- 2 tablespoons water
- 2 cups of shredded cheddar cheese
- ½-cup all-purpose flour
- ¼ cup butter or margarine
- ½-cup fine dry bread crumbs
- Vegetable or Canola oil for deep-frying

DIRECTIONS: Skin chicken breasts, remove and discard bones from chicken. Place each piece of chicken between two pieces of clear plastic wrap; pound to 1/8-inch thickness, working from center. Remove plastic wrap. Sprinkle each piece of chicken with some parsley and onion. Season with salt. Place cheese on each chicken piece. Fold in sides; roll up jelly roll-style, pressing ends to seal. In shallow dish, combine eggs and water. Place flour in another shallow dish. Roll chicken in flour to coat, and then dip in egg mixture. Coat with crumbs. Cover; chill at least 1 hour. Heat ¼-cup butter or margarine in large skillet. Fry chicken rolls on all sides until brown. Transfer to a 12x7 1/2x2 inch baking dish. Heat oven to 400 degrees, for 15 to 18 minutes. Add a few chicken rolls. Fry for 5 minutes or until golden. Remove with tongs; drain on paper towels. Repeat with remaining rolls.

CHEESY STUFFED TURKEY MEATBALL AND SPAGHETTI

INGREDIENTS:

    1 lb ground turkey
    ½-cup Italian seasoned dry bread crumbs
    1 egg
    2 ounces mozzarella cheese, cut into 12 (1/2 inch) cubes
    1 jar (1lb. 10 oz.) pasta sauce
    8 ounces spaghetti, cooked and drained

DIRECTIONS: In medium bowl, combine ground turkey, breadcrumbs and egg; shape into 12 meatballs. Press 1 cheese cube into each meatball, enclosing completely. In 3- quart saucepan, bring pasta sauce to a boil over medium high heat. Gently stir in uncooked meatballs. Reduce heat to low and simmer covered, stirring occasionally, 20 minutes or until meatballs are done. Serve over hot spaghetti.

PENNE WITH PARMESAN

INGREDIENTS:

2 tablespoons butter or margarine
2 cloves garlic, minced
1 ½ cups (about 4oz.) thinly sliced fresh mushrooms
¾ cup (about 2oz.) ground turkey
½-cup light cream
2 2/3 cups Penne Pasta, uncooked
¼ cup grated Parmesan cheese divided
¼ cup chopped fresh parsley

INSTRUCTIONS: In a large skillet over medium heat, melt butter, garlic and mushrooms. Cook 3 minutes or until mushrooms are tender, stirring frequently. Add ground turkey, milk and cream; heat to boiling. Reduce heat to medium; simmer, uncovered, until mixture is reduced by half, about 6 minutes. Meanwhile, cook pasta according to package direction and drain. Remove sauce from heat; add 3tablespoons Parmesan cheese and parsley. Toss hot pasta and sauce; sprinkle with remaining cheese. 4 servings.

STUFFED CHICKEN BREASTS PARMESAN

INGREDIENTS:
- ¾ cup shredded mozzarella cheese
- 2 tablespoons minced parsley
- 4 small skinless, boneless chicken breast halves
- ½ cup grated parmesan
- ¼-cup flour
- 2 tablespoons olive oil
- 2 cups bottled marinara sauce
- 1 10-ounce package of spinach

DIRECTIONS: Preheat oven to 400 degrees. In a small bowl, stir together mozzarella and parsley. Dividing evenly, sprinkle mozzarella mixture down center of each chicken cutlet to within an inch of the far tip. Spread spinach down center of chicken cutlet as well. Roll up and secure with toothpicks. In a shallow bowl, combine ¼ cup of parmesan and the flour. Dredge each chicken roll in parmesan/flour mixture, pressing to adhere. In a medium nonstick skillet, heat oil over medium heat. Add chicken rolls and cook, turning, 6 to 8 minutes or until golden brown and crispy on all sides. Remove toothpicks. Place 1 cup of marinara sauce in 8-inch square baking pan. Add chicken rolls. Top with remaining 1-cup marinara sauce and sprinkle with remaining ¼-cup parmesan. Bake for 15 minutes or until sauce is bubbly. Let stand 5 minutes before serving.

Black Bean Quesadillas

Ingredients:
Non-stick cooking spray
4 (8-inch) flour tortillas
¾ cup (3 ounces) shredded Monterey Jack or Cheddar Cheese
½ cup rinsed and drained canned black beans
2 green onions with tops, sliced
¼ cup minced fresh cilantro
½-teaspoon ground cumin
½-cup salsa
2 tablespoon plus 2-teaspoon sour cream

Directions: Preheat oven to 450 degrees. Spray large nonstick baking sheet with cooking spray. Place 2 tortillas on prepared baking sheet; sprinkle each with half the cheese. Combine beans, green onions, cilantro and cumin in small bowl; mix lightly. Spoon bean mixture evenly over cheese; top with remaining tortillas. Coat tops with cooking spray. Bake 10 to 12 minutes or until cheese is melted and tortillas are lightly browned. Cut into wedges; top each wedge with 1 tablespoon of salsa and 1-teaspoon sour cream.

Black Bean Tostadas

INGREDIENTS:

    1 cup rinsed and drained canned black beans, mashed
    2-teaspoon chili powder
    Nonstick cooking spray
    4 (8-inch) corn tortillas
    1 cup washed, torn romaine lettuce leaves
    1 cup chopped seeded tomato
    ½ cup chopped onion
    ½ cup plain nonfat yogurt
    2 jalapeno peppers, seeded and finely chopped

DIRECTIONS: Combine beans and chili powder in small saucepan. Cook 5 minutes over medium heat or until heated through, stirring occasionally. Spray large nonstick skillet with cooking spray. Heat over medium heat until hot. Sprinkle tortillas with water; place in skillet, one at a time. Cook 20 to 30 seconds or until hot and pliable, turning once. Spread bean mixture evenly over tortillas; layer with lettuce, tomato, onion, yogurt and peppers. Garnish with cilantro, sliced tomatoes and peppers, if desired. Serve immediately.

SESAME CHICKEN SALAD WONTON CUPS

INGREDIENTS:
   Nonstick cooking spray
   20 (3-inch) wonton wrappers
   1-tablespoon sesame seeds
   2 small boneless skinless chicken breasts (about 8 ounces)
   1-cup fresh green beans, cut diagonally into ½-inch pieces.
   ¼ cup reduced calorie mayonnaise
   1 tablespoon chopped fresh cilantro (optional)
   2 teaspoons honey
   1-teaspoon reduced-sodium soy sauce
   1/8 teaspoon ground red pepper

DIRECTIONS: Preheat oven to 350 degrees. Spray muffin pan with nonstick cooking spray. Press 1 wonton wrapper into each muffin cup; bake 8 to 10 minutes or until golden brown. Cool in pan on wire rack before filling. Place sesame seeds in shallow baking pan. Bake 5 minutes or until lightly toasted, stirring occasionally. Set aside to cool. Meanwhile, bring 2 cups water to a boil in medium saucepan. Add chicken. Reduce heat to low; cover. Simmer 10 minutes or until chicken is no longer pink in center, adding green beans after 7 minutes. Drain. Finely chop chicken, place in medium bowl. Add green beans and remaining ingredients; mix lightly. Spoon lightly rounded tablespoonful of chicken mixture into each wonton cup.

HERBED POTATO CHIPS

INGREDIENTS:
Nonstick olive oil flavored cooking spray
2 medium sized red potatoes (about ½ pound), unpeeled
1-tablespoon olive oil
2 teaspoons dried dill weed, thyme or rosemary
¼-teaspoon garlic salt
1/8 teaspoon black pepper

DIRECTIONS: Preheat oven to 450 degrees. Spray large nonstick baking sheets with cooking spray; set aside. Cut potatoes crosswise into very thin slices, about 1/16 inch thick. Pat dry with paper towels. Arrange potato slices in single layer on prepared baking sheets; coat potatoes with cooking spray. Bake 10 minutes; turn slices over. Brush with oil. Combine dill, garlic salt, and pepper in small bowl; sprinkle evenly onto potato slices. Continue baking 5 to 10 minutes or until potatoes are golden brown. Cool on baking sheets.

Bar-BQ Shrimp

Ingredients:

    8 pounds of large shrimp (devined)
    ¼ pound of butter
    1 cup of olive oil
    2-8 ounce bottles chili sauce
    3 tablespoons of Worcestershire sauce
    2 lemons, sliced
    4 cloves of garlic, chopped
    3 tablespoons of lemon juice
    1 tablespoon of parsley, chopped
    3 teaspoons of red pepper
    1 teaspoon of Tabasco sauce
    Salt and pepper to taste

DIRECTIONS: Wash shrimp. Spread out in shallow pans. Combine ingredients in saucepan over low heat and pour over shrimp. Refrigerate. Baste and turn shrimp every 30 minutes while refrigerated for several hours. Bake at 300 degrees for 30 minutes, turning shrimp at 10-minute intervals. Serve in soup bowl with French bread to dip in sauce.

SHRIMP AND WILD RICE CASSEROLE

INGREDIENTS:
- ½ cup of thinly sliced onions
- ¼ cup of thinly sliced green pepper
- ½ cup of mushrooms
- 1 tablespoon of Worcestershire sauce
- 1 teaspoon of curry powder
- 4 drops of Tabasco
- 2 cups of cooked wild rice
- 2 pounds of cooked shrimp (devined)
- 2 cups of thin cream sauce

DIRECTIONS: In making cream sauce, use chicken broth instead of milk. Sauté onions, pepper, mushrooms in butter, add seasonings, rice, shrimp and sauce. Place in casserole and bake at 325 degree until heated through.

CREOLE SHRIMP

INGREDIENTS:

    4 cups of sliced onions

    2 cloves of garlic, minced

    ¼ cup of olive oil or salad oil

    4 cups of coarsely chopped peeled tomatoes (canned tomato wedges can be used)

    3 cups coarsely chopped green peppers (about 3 medium peppers)

    1 cup sliced mushrooms

    2-8 ounce cans of tomato sauce

    ¼ cup of dry white wine

    2-teaspoon salt

    ½ teaspoon of thyme

    ¼-teaspoon pepper

    3 pounds of shrimp, cooked and cleaned (devined)

    1 bay leaf

DIRECTIONS: Add onion and garlic to oil in large fry pan. Cook until tender, not brown. Add tomatoes, green peppers, mushrooms and tomato sauce; stir and cook 5 minutes. Add wine, salt, thyme, pepper and bay leaf. Mix well. Simmer uncovered to cook vegetables and blend flavors, about 20 minutes. Add shrimp; heat well. Serve over rice pilaf or pasta.

CHINESE FRIED RICE

INGREDIENTS:

    1-cup regular long grain rice (or 3 cups cold, cooked rice)
    6 eggs
    ¼-teaspoon salt
    Olive oil
    ¼ cup of chopped red peppers
    ¼ cup of bean sprouts
    ½ cup of chopped tofu
    1-tablespoon soy sauce
    2 tablespoons chopped green onions

DIRECTIONS: Prepare rice as label directs. Refrigerate until well chilled. In medium bowl with fork, beat eggs and salt lightly. In 12-inch skillet over high heat, heat 3 tablespoons of olive oil until very hot. Pour in egg mixture, using a spoon, stirring quickly and constantly until eggs are the size of peas and leave side of pan. Reduce heat to low. Push eggs to one side of skillet. In same skillet, gently stir rice, tofu, bean sprouts, and 2 tablespoons olive oil until rice is well coated. Add soy sauce; gently stir to mix all ingredients in skillet; heat through. Spoon fried rice into warm bowl; sprinkle with green onions.

Jalapeño Chicken Rolls

INGREDIENTS:

8 or more skinless and boneless chicken breasts pounded flat

1- 16 ounce bakery type breadcrumbs or regular bread blended

4 eggs with ¼ cup of French dressing, added and beaten well

Vegetable or canola oil for frying

STUFFING:

8 ounces of grated cheddar cheese

8 ounces of mozzarella cheese

¼-cup Parmesan cheese

2 bunches of green onions thinly sliced

¼-cup whole oregano leaves

spicy seasoning salt to taste

½-cup celery thinly sliced

1 jar of jalapeno cheese whiz (to be added to above mixture when stuffing chicken breasts)

Gravy:

2 cans golden mushroom soup

½ cup cooking wine (red or white)

2 cups chicken broth

Mix and heat well (set aside)

DIRECTIONS: Take flatten chicken breasts, place stuffing mix on each piece. Roll up and tuck in end. Dip each roll in egg mixture. Roll each in breadcrumbs. Drop each roll in hot oil and brown quickly. Place each roll in covered roasting pan and bake for 30 minutes at 350 degrees. Pour beated gravy over roll and return to oven and bake for 30 minutes more. Serve with rice pilaf.

Turkey Stroganoff

INGREDIENTS:
- 2 tablespoon of flour
- 1 ½ pound of turkey cut into cubes
- 3 tablespoons of vegetable oil
- Salt and pepper to taste
- 8 ounce sliced mushrooms
- ½ cup of red wine
- 1 cup of sour cream
- 1 pound of cooked egg noodles

DIRECTIONS: Cook egg noodles and set aside. Coat turkey cubes with flour, shake off excess. Heat oil in 10" skillet and add meat to pan to sear the turkey. Reduce heat; add salt and pepper, mushrooms and red wine. Simmer 8-10 minutes. Add sour cream and blend until mixture is smooth and creamy.

Cook 1 minute. Add cooked egg noodles and toss to coat.

Serve with garlic bread or breadsticks.

GRILLED EGGPLANT

INGREDIENTS:

    1 large eggplant
    1/3 cup butter or margarine, melted
    ½-teaspoon garlic salt
    ½ teaspoon of Italian seasoning
    ¼ teaspoon of salt
    1/8 teaspoon of pepper

DIRECTIONS: Peel the eggplant, and then cut into ¾-inch slices. Combine butter, garlic salt, and Italian seasoning; stir well. Brush eggplant slices with butter mixture, and sprinkle with salt and pepper. Place eggplant about 3 to 4 inches from coals. Grill over medium coals 10 minutes or until tender, turning and basting occasionally.

EGGPLANT CASSEROLE

INGREDIENTS:

- 1 large eggplant
- 2-tablespoon milk
- 1 large onion, chopped
- 2 eggs, well beaten
- 1-cup cracker crumbs
- 1-cup dry bread crumbs
- ½ cup of butter or margarine, melted
- ½ teaspoon of pepper
- 1 teaspoon of salt
- ½ cup of milk
- 1 cup of shredded extra sharp cheddar cheese, divided
- ½ cup of grated parmesan cheese
- 1 teaspoon dried whole oregano
- 1 bay leaf, crumbled
- 2 medium tomatoes cut into ½-inch slices

DIRECTIONS: Peel eggplant, and cut into 1/2 inch slices. Dissolve ½-cup salt in water; add eggplant, and soak for 30 minutes. Drain well, and pat dry. Combine 2 eggs and 2-tablespoon milk, mixing well. Dip eggplant in mixture, and coat with cracker crumbs. Fry a few at a time in ½ cup of margarine, just until browned, turning once. Repeat until all are browned; drain on paper towels. Sauté chopped onions and green peppers until tender. Stir in salt, pepper, oregano, and bay leaf. Layer one/third of eggplant, half each of tomato slices and cheddar cheese in a greased 13x9x2 inch baking dish. Repeat layers. Place remaining eggplant on top, and sprinkle with parmesan cheese. Combine 2 eggs and ½-cup milk, mixing well; pour over casserole. Bake at 375 degrees for 35 minutes.

CHICKEN ENCHILADAS

INGREDIENTS:
- 1 lb. ground chicken or ground turkey
- 1 lb. Monterey Jack Cheese, shredded
- 1 lb. Cheddar Cheese
- 1-cup sour cream
- ¼ teaspoon
- 1-teaspoon chili powder
- 1/8 teaspoon ground red pepper
- 10 6-inch flour tortillas
- 1 ½ cup of enchilada sauce
- ½ cup sliced black olives
- ¼ cup minced green onion

DIRECTIONS: Combine chicken breast, 2 cups of Monterey Jack Cheese, 2 cups of Cheddar cheese, sour cream, and seasonings; mix well. Spread ¼ cup of chicken mixture on each tortilla; roll up tightly. Pour ½-cup enchilada sauce on bottom of 12"x 8" baking dish. Place tortillas in baking dish, seam side down; top with remaining enchilada sauce and cheese. Bake at 350 degree for 20 minutes, or until thoroughly heated. Top with olives and green onion.

EGGPLANT SANDWICH MELT

INGREDIENTS:

1 can tomato with garden herb condensed soup
1/4 cup fat free, low sodium vegetable broth
3 sandwich-size English muffins, split and toasted
Vegetable cooking spray
1 small eggplant, cut crosswise into 1 inch slices and grilled
½ cup roasted red bell pepper strips, drained
½ cup shredded mozzarella cheese (any cheese)

DIRECTIONS: In a small bowl, combine soup and vegetable broth; mix well. Set aside. Place toasted muffin halves in single layer in shallow baking dish sprayed with vegetable cooking spray. Spread 1-tablespoon soup mixture on each muffin half. Top each muffin half with 1 slice eggplant and 1 bell pepper strip. Pour remaining soup mixture evenly over sandwiches and sprinkle with cheese. Cover and bake at 350 degrees for 10 minutes or until cheese is melted and sandwiches are heated through.

Meatless Sloppy Joes

Ingredients:

    2 cups thinly sliced onions
    2 cups chopped green bell peppers
    2 cloves garlic, finely chopped
    2 tablespoons ketchup
    1-tablespoon mustard
    2 cup of crumbled tofu
    1 can (8 ounces) tomato sauce
    1-teaspoon chili powder
    2 sandwich rolls, halved

DIRECTIONS: Coat skillet with oil, add onions, peppers and garlic. Cook and stir 5 minutes over medium heat. Stir in ketchup, mustard, sauce, and chili powder. Cook 5 minutes, stirring frequently. Serve on rolls.

GRILLED CHEESE 'N' TOMATO SANDWICHES

INGREDIENTS:

   8 slices whole wheat bread, divided
   6 ounces part-skim mozzarella cheese or cheddar cheese,
   cut into 4 slices
   1 large tomato, cut into 8 thin slices
   1/3 cup yellow cornmeal
   2 tablespoon grated parmesan cheese
   1 teaspoon dried basil leaves
   ½-cup eggs
   ¼-cup skim milk
   2 tablespoons corn oil spread, divided
   1 cup low-salt tomato sauce, heated

DIRECTIONS: On each of 4 bread slices, place 1 cheese slice and 2 tomato slices; top with remaining bread slices. Combine cornmeal, parmesan cheese and basil on waxed paper. In shallow bowl, combine eggbeaters and milk. Melt 1-tablespoon corn oil spread in large nonstick skillet. Dip sandwiches in egg mixture; coat with cornmeal mixture. Transfer 2 sandwiches to skillet. Cook sandwiches for 3 minutes on each side or until golden. Repeat using remaining spread and sandwiches. Cut sandwiches in half; serve warm with tomato sauce for dipping.

Spinach-Cheddar Squares

Ingredients:
- 1 ½ cups eggs
- ¾-cup skim milk
- 1 tablespoon dried onion flakes
- 1 tablespoon grated parmesan cheese
- ¼-teaspoon garlic powder
- 1/8 teaspoon ground black pepper
- ¼-cup plain dry bread crumbs
- ¾ cup shredded fat-free cheddar cheese, divided
- 1 (10-ounce) package frozen chopped spinach, thawed and well drained
- ¼ cup diced pimientos

Directions: In medium bowl, combine eggbeaters, milk, onion flakes, parmesan cheese, garlic powder and pepper; set aside. Sprinkle bread crumbs evenly into bottom of lightly greased 8x8x2 inch baking dish. Top with ½-cup cheddar cheese and spinach. Pour egg mixture evenly over spinach; top with remaining cheddar and pimentos. Bake at 350 degrees for 35 to 40 minutes or until knife inserted in center comes our clean. Let stand 10 minutes before cutting and serving.

Glazed Acorn Squash Rings

INGREDIENTS:
- 1 large acorn squash
- 1/3 cup orange juice
- ½ cup firmly packed brown sugar
- ¼ cup butter or margarine
- 2 teaspoon grated lemon rind
- 1/8 teaspoon salt
- Parsley (optional)
- Orange slice (optional)

DIRECTIONS: Cut squash into ¾-inch thick slices; remove seeds and membrane. Arrange squash in lightly greased shallow baking dish. Pour orange juice over squash. Cover; bake at 350 degrees for 30 minutes. Combine next 5 ingredients in saucepan. Bring to a boil; reduce heat, and simmer 5 minutes. Pour mixture of squash. Bake, uncovered an additional 15 to 20 minutes or until squash is tender, basting occasionally. Garnish with orange slices and parsley, if desired.

Parmesan Fried Fish

INGREDIENTS:
    1-pound fresh fish fillets
    ¼-cup all-purpose flour
    Dash garlic salt
    1 beaten egg
    ¼-cup milk
    ½ cup finely crushed crackers (14 crackers)
    2 tablespoons grated parmesan cheese
    2 tablespoons parsley
    ½ cup canola oil

DIRECTIONS: Rinse fish and pat dry with paper toweling. Combine flour and garlic salt; set aside. Blend egg and milk; set aside. Combine cracker crumbs, parmesan, and parsley. Coat fish with flour mixture. Dip in egg mixture then coat with crumb mixture. In large skillet, add fish in a single layer to hot oil. Fry over medium heat for 4 to 5 minutes per side or until fish browns and flakes easily when tested with a fork. Drain on paper toweling and serve. Garnish with lemon slice and parsley, if desired.

Marinated Carrots

Ingredients:

    ½-cup vinegar
    1 onion sliced thin
    1 green pepper
    1 can tomato soup
    ½-cup vegetable oil
    1 teaspoon of dry mustard
    1-teaspoon Worchester sauce
    1 lb bag of sliced carrots

DIRECTIONS: Baste sliced carrots until barely tender, alternate sliced carrots, pepper and onion in a bowl. Boil other ingredients about 20-25 minutes until mix thicken. Pour over carrots mix and marinate at least 12 hours before serving.

IMPERIAL CHICKEN ROLLUPS

INGREDIENTS:

¾ cup butter or margarine, melted

2 cloves of garlic, pressed

1-cup fine dry breadcrumbs

2/3 cup of grated Parmesan Cheese

¼ cup minced fresh parsley

¼-teaspoon pepper

4 whole chicken breasts, split, skinned, and boned

Juice of 2 lemons

Paprika

DIRECTIONS: Combine butter and garlic; stir well, and set aside. Combine breadcrumbs, cheese, parsley, salt, and pepper; stir well. Dip chicken in butter mixture, and coat with breadcrumb mixture. Fold long sides of chicken together; bring short ends over and secure with a toothpick. Place chicken rolls seam side down in a greased 13x9x2 inch pan; sprinkle with lemon juice and paprika. Bake at 350 degrees for 1 hour or until down.

Baked Sliced Mushroom

Ingredients:
- 1/3 cup chopped onions
- ¼ cup butter or margarine
- 3 eggs beaten
- 8 ounces sliced fresh mushrooms
- 2 tablespoons chopped green pepper
- 1¼ cups milk
- 1 ½ cups bread cubes
- ½-teaspoon salt
- ¼-teaspoon thyme
- Dash of pepper

DIRECTIONS: Sauté mushrooms. Add onions, green pepper, and sauté very lightly in butter. Combine with other ingredients and pour into 5 cup buttered baking dish. Bake in 350-degree oven for 50-60 minutes.

BAKED EGGPLANT ROLLUP

INGREDIENTS:
  1 ¼-pounds eggplant
  1 egg
  ¼-cup milk
  1 cup dried breadcrumbs
  Olive oil
  1 -15 ounces can of tomato sauce
  ¼ teaspoon of salt
  ¼ teaspoon of pepper
  Oregano leaves
  ½ pound of Monterey Jack Cheese
  1 cup of ricotta cheese

DIRECTIONS: Use a well-sharpened knife. Slice eggplant lengthwise into twelve 1/8 inch thick slices. Preheat broiler. In a pie plate, mix egg and milk. Place bread crumbs onwaxed paper. Dip eggplant slice in egg mixture, then coat with breadcrumbs. Brush 15 ½ inch by 10 ½-inch jelly roll pan with 3 tablespoon olive oil. Place half of eggplant slice in pan, arranging them so they fit in one layer. Broil eggplant 5 to 7 minutes until tender and lightly browned on both sides; remove to plate. Repeat with 3 more tablespoons oil and remaining eggplant. In bowl, mix tomato sauce, salt, pepper, and ¼-teaspoon oregano; set aside. After browning eggplant, roll slice jellyroll fashion, starting at narrow end, around cheese. Turn oven to 350 degrees. Shred Monterey Jack cheese. In a bowl, mix ricotta, ¼-teaspoon oregano, and all but 2 tablespoons shredded Monterey jack. Spoon about 2 tablespoons cheese mixture in ½-inch wide strip on each eggplant slice; roll. Spoon some tomato sauce mixture into bottom of 2-quart baking dish. Place eggplant rolls, seam-side down, in sauce in baking dish; top with remaining sauce. Bake 30 minutes or until heated through. Sprinkle eggplant rolls with remaining Monterey Jack; return to oven and heat just until cheese melts.

PIZZA WITH A FRENCH ACCENT

INGREDIENTS:

    1 package (1 lb., 4oz.) frozen diced Potatoes with Onions

    ½ tsp. basil

    1- 12-inch pre-baked pizza crust

    1 medium tomato, chopped

    1 jar (6oz) marinated artichokes, drained and chopped (optional)

    1 cup of chopped turkey (or cooked chicken)

    1 cup (4oz) shredded mozzarella

DIRECTIONS: Heat oven at 425 degrees. Cooked potatoes, sprinkle with basil. Place crust on an ungreased pizza pan or cookie sheet. Arrange potatoes, tomato, artichokes and chicken (or turkey) on crust. Top with cheese. Bake for 10-12 minutes or until heated thoroughly and cheese is melted. To serve, cut in wedges.

STUFFED FLOUNDER

INGREDIENTS:

4-pound flounder
Dressing Stuffing
2 slices whole grain bread
½ cup fresh bean sprouts
¼ cup of diced, sautéed celery
¼ cup of diced, sautéed onion
¼ cup of unprocessed bran
1 teaspoon low-sodium vegetable seasoning
½-teaspoon sage
¼ cup chopped fresh mushrooms
2 egg whites
2 to 3 tablespoons chicken broth

DIRECTIONS: Place fish on a large piece of foil in a large open pan; set aside. Stuffing: Chop bread finely; add all other ingredients with enough chicken broth to hold together. Stuff fish, bake at 400 degree; allowing 12 minutes per pound. A 3-ounce serving of fish is about 150 calories and ¼ cup stuffing about 30 calories.

Chicago Gumbo -(My original personal recipe)

Ingredients:
- 1 box of Penne pasta
- 1 can of Black beans
- 1 can of Chickpeas
- 1 can of Vegetarian beans
- 1 bag of Spanish rice (or brown rice)
- 1 bag of mixed vegetables
- 2 bottles of Garden combination pasta sauce
- Parmesan Cheese
- 1 lb of ground turkey

DIRECTIONS: Cooking rice: 2 cups of water (bring to a boil), 1 tbsp. of margarine. Cook for 7 minutes or until rice is tender, then let stand until sauce thickens (about 2-3 minutes). Cooking pasta: 4 cups of water (bring to a boil). Cook pasta for about 7 minutes or until tender. Cooking vegetables: place vegetables in a microwave safe container with a little water and cook for 4 minutes. Cooking ground turkey: a large skillet sprayed with cooking spray or olive oil, and cook until brown. In a big pot: After the pasta and rice is done and drained. Sprinkle parmesan cheese over it. Add mixed vegetables, turkey, add the black beans, chickpeas, and vegetarian beans in the mixture. Mix all together over a low heat, add Garden Combination Pasta Sauce, add cooked rice to mixture. Serve.

FIESTA BAKED POTATO

INGREDIENTS:

1 large-size baking potato (preferably russet), well scrubbed.

3 tablespoons prepared salsa

¼ cup canned black beans, drained and rinsed

2 tablespoons shredded cheddar cheese

1 tablespoon chopped green onion

1 teaspoon of onion flakes

1 teaspoon of garlic flakes

DIRECTIONS: To bake potato: Heat oven to 400 degrees. With fork, pierce skin in several places. Bake 40 to 50 minutes (depending on microwave power and size of potato) until tender when tested with fork. Slit potato; fluff with fork. Place on baking sheet or microwave-safe dish. Top with salsa, beans and cheese. Bake or microwave just until cheese melts, about 1 to 2 minutes. Sprinkle with onions and, if desired add sour cream and pickled peppers. Preparation time: 5 minutes. Total time: 55 minutes in conventional oven; 15 minutes in microwave oven.

Honey Dip Chicken

INGREDIENTS:
- 2-3 lbs. chicken pieces
- 1 tablespoon onion flakes
- 1 tablespoon garlic flakes
- Honey

DIRECTIONS: Place chicken pieces, skin side down, on meat rack. Brush with honey and sprinkle with onion and garlic flakes. Cover with waxed paper and cook for 7 minutes per pound, on full power. Halfway through cooking, turn chicken pieces over, brush with honey, and sprinkle with onion and garlic flakes. Cover with foil and let stand for 10 minutes.

BURGER MEDLEY

INGREDIENTS:

1 lb. ground turkey or ground chicken

½ cup chopped green pepper

½ cup chopped onion

1 ½ - 2 cups water

1-15 oz. can tomato sauce with pieces

1-8 oz. can whole kernel corn, un-drained

4 oz. elbow macaroni

1/8 tsp. hot pepper sauce

1 cup corn chips, crushed

DIRECTIONS: Combine ground turkey or chicken, green pepper, and onion in 3-quart casserole. Cook in microwave for 4 ½ to 5 ½ minutes, stirring several times; and drain if necessary. Stir in water, tomato sauce, corn, macaroni, and hot pepper sauce. Heat, covered on full power for 10 minutes and then 50% power for 8-9 minutes, stir once during cooking. Stand for 10 minutes. Serve.

Spinach Casserole

INGREDIENTS:

    1-10 oz. pkg. frozen chopped spinach
    2 eggs, beaten
    2 tbsp. milk
    ¼-cup cottage cheese
    ¼ cup grated sharp cheddar cheese
    1/8 tsp. salt
    1-cup herb seasoned stuffing mix

DIRECTIONS: Remove waxed wrapper from spinach and pierce box several times. Place on paper plate and cook in microwave for 3 minutes or until spinach can be separated; drained well. Combine all ingredients in bowl and then into greased 1 quart casserole dish. Cook in microwave for 7-9 minutes. Let stand for 2-3 minutes.

Turkey Burgers

Ingredients:
- 1 pound ground turkey breast
- 1-cup whole wheat bread crumbs
- 1 egg white
- ½ teaspoon dried sage leaves
- ½ teaspoon dried marjoram leaves
- ¼-teaspoon salt
- ½ teaspoon granulated garlic
- ½ tablespoon onion (granulated)
- ¼-teaspoon canola oil
- 4 whole grain sandwich rolls, split in half
- ¼ cup of barbecue sauce

Directions: Combine turkey, breadcrumbs, egg white, sage, marjoram, salt and pepper in large bowl until well blended. Shape into 4 patties. Heat oil in large nonstick skillet over medium-high heat until hot, add patties. Cook 10 minutes or until patties are no longer pink in centers, turning once. Place one patty on bottom half of each roll. Spoon 1- tablespoon barbecue sauce over top of each burger. Serve with lettuce and tomato and garnish with carrot slice, if desired.

SALMON CAKES

INGREDIENTS:

14 ounce can salmon, drained and picked over (the bones are edible, but it's advisable to remove them for the safety of small children)

¼ cup grated or finely chopped onion

¼ cup finely chopped bell pepper

½-teaspoon salt (optional)

½-teaspoon ground black pepper

1 large egg, slightly beaten

½ teaspoon of garlic powder

1-cup bread crumbs

½-cup canola oil

OPTIONAL GARNISHES: tartar sauce, lemon wedges, capers. Makes 5 cakes. Preparation time: 15 minutes. Total time: 25 minutes.

DIRECTIONS: Place in large bowl; salmon, onion, bell pepper, salt, pepper, garlic powder, ½ cup of bread crumbs, and egg. Mix well, divide mixture into 5 portions; shape each into patty. Spread bread crumbs on large plate or waxed paper; dredge patties with bread crumbs to evenly coat. Heat oil in large, heavy bottom skillet over medium high heat. Add salmon patties; cook until golden brown on underside, about 3 minutes. Turn cakes over and continue cooking until browned on other side, about 2 minutes longer. Transfer as cooked to plate with paper towels to briefly drain. Serve with tartar sauce, lemon wedges and capers. Do not over cook.

BAR-BE-CUPS

INGREDIENTS:
- ¾ lb. ground turkey
- ½-cup barbecue sauce
- 1 tbsp. instant minced onion
- 1 (8oz.) can refrigerator biscuits
- ½ cup shredded cheddar cheese

DIRECTIONS: Brown ground turkey and drain. Add barbecue sauce and onion. Set aside. Place 1 biscuit in each ungreased muffin cup. Press dough up and the sides to the edge of the cup. Spoon meat mixture into cups. Sprinkle with cheese. Bake at 400 degrees for 10 minutes or golden brown.

Grilled Chicken and Vegetables

Ingredients:

2 lbs. fresh vegetables ex. red and yellow bell peppers, zucchini, yellow squash, eggplant, onion, sliced portabella mushrooms.

¾ lb. boneless, skinless chicken breasts.

2 Tbsp. olive oil

¼ cup Italian dressing

¾ cup Parmesan Cheese

1 tsp. garlic powder

8oz. (1/2 pkg.) pasta, cooked and drained.

DIRECTIONS: Cut vegetables into large pieces for grilling. Brush chicken and vegetables with oil. Grill over medium coals 8 to 12 minutes or until cooked through and tender, turning occasionally. Slice chicken and vegetables into bite-size pieces and place in large serving bowl. Mix the dressing, cheese and garlic powder together. Add pasta and toss to coat. Serve immediately. Makes 4 servings, Prep. Time: 20 minutes.

SHELLS AND PEPPERS

INGREDIENTS:

    2 tbsp olive oil
    1- ½ cup thinly sliced green pepper strips
    1 cup thinly sliced sweet red or yellow pepper strips
    1 cup thinly sliced onion
    1 tbsp. finely chopped garlic or ¾ tsp garlic powder
    3- ½ cups (28 oz. can) whole tomatoes, undrained and chopped.
    2 tsp. dried Italian seasoning
    Salt and ground black pepper to taste
    3 cups medium pasta shells, uncooked
    Grated Parmesan Cheese

DIRECTIONS: In large skillet over medium heat, heat oil; add peppers, onion and garlic. Cook 10 minutes, stirring occasionally, or until lightly browned. Stir in tomatoes with juice and seasonings; heat to boiling. Reduce heat; simmer 15 minutes. Meanwhile, cook pasta according to package directions; drain. Toss hot pasta and sauce; sprinkle with cheese. Makes 6 servings (1 cup each).

TAMALE PIE

INGREDIENTS:
- 1 large chopped onion
- 1 can cream style corn
- 1 small can of sliced mushrooms
- ¼ cup of grated cheese
- 1 tablespoon of olive oil
- 1 can of tamales peeled and cut in bite size pieces
- 1 can of tomato soup ½ cup of pitted olives
- ¼ teaspoon of black pepper

DIRECTIONS: Sauté onions in olive oil, until brown. Then add all other ingredients, saving a little cheese for topping. Place in a casserole, heat thoroughly, add rest of grated cheese and let it melt.

Chicken Tetrazzini

INGREDIENTS:

 3 cups (8oz.) pasta, uncooked
 2 cups cooked chicken strips, 1-inch long
 ¼ cup butter or margarine
 1 cup chopped sweet red pepper
 ½ cup sliced green onion
 ¼-cup all-purpose flour
 2 cups half-and-half or milk
 1-3/4 cups (14-1/2 oz. can) chicken broth
 1/3 cup dry sherry, milk or water
 ½ cup grated Parmesan cheese, divided

DIRECTIONS: Heat oven to 350 degrees. Cook pasta according to package directions for 7 minutes; drain. In 3-quart baking dish, stir together hot pasta and chicken. Meanwhile, in 4-quart saucepan over medium-high heat, melt butter; add red pepper and onion. Cook 5 minutes, stirring occasionally, or until red pepper is tender; reduce heat to medium. Stir in flour; cook 1 minute, stirring constantly. Stir in half-and-half, chicken broth and sherry. Cook, stirring frequently until mixture boils and thickens. Remove from heat; stir in ¼-cup parmesan cheese. Add salt to taste. Pour sauce over pasta mixture; sprinkle with remaining cheese. Bake 20 minutes or until hot and bubbly.

Fried Green Tomatoes

INGREDIENTS:

> 6 large green tomatoes (about 3 pounds)
> 2 tablespoon of lemon juice
> ½ cup of cornmeal
> 2 teaspoons of freshly ground black pepper
> Nonstick cooking spray

DIRECTIONS: Slice each tomato into ½-inch thick slices. Sprinkle the lemon juice on the tomatoes. Mix the cornmeal and black pepper in a plastic bag. Put the tomato slice into the bag and shake well. Coat a cast iron skillet or nonstick sauté pan with nonstick cooking spray. Fry the tomatoes, over medium-high heat, until they are light brown on each side.

MARY-ANN'S SURPRISE

INGREDIENTS:

    6 to 8 slices turkey bacon, diced
    1 medium onion, chopped
    ½ cup sliced celery
    ¼ tsp. thyme leaves, crushed
    2 16-ounces packages frozen black-eyed peas
    3 cups water
    1-cup rice
    2 tbsp. chopped parsley
    1 tsp. salt, optional
    ½ tsp. crushed red pepper

DIRECTIONS: Cook onion and celery with turkey bacon and thyme until tender; drain. Stir in remaining ingredients. Bring to a boil. Reduce heat; cover and simmer for 20 minutes or until rice is tender.

Spicy Oven-Fried Catfish

Ingredients:
    4 dressed farm-raised catfish (about 7 ounces each)
    ¼ cup yellow cornmeal
    ¼-cup dry bread crumbs
    ½ tsp. salt, optional
    ½ tsp. paprika
    ½ tsp. garlic powder
    1/8 tsp. cayenne pepper
    1/8 tsp. ground thyme
    ½-cup skim milk
    ¼ cup margarine, melted

DIRECTIONS: Move oven rack to position slightly above middle oven. Heat oven to 450 degrees. Combine cornmeal, breadcrumbs, salt, paprika, garlic powder, cayenne pepper, and thyme. Dip fish into milk; coat with cornmeal mixture. Place in 13x9x2-inch rectangular pan coated with vegetable cooking spray. Pour margarine over fish. Bake uncovered until fish flakes very easily with fork, about 15 to 20 minutes. Yields 4 servings

Collard Greens

INGREDIENTS:
    1 pound smoked turkey parts (optional)
    1 ½ quart water
    1 to 2 hot pepper pods or 1 tsp. crushed red pepper
    3 cloves garlic, minced
    4 pounds fresh collard greens or mixed greens
    1 medium onion, chopped
    2 celery stalks, chopped
    1 small green pepper, chopped
    1 tbsp. vegetable or olive oil
    Salt and pepper

DIRECTIONS: Place turkey parts in Dutch oven or large saucepan; add water, pepper pods and garlic. Cover; bring to boil; reduce heat to low and simmer 30 minutes. Break off and discard stems of collards. Wash leaves thoroughly. Slice leaves into bite-size pieces by rolling several leaves together and slicing in ¼-inch strips. Add collards, onion, celery, green pepper, oil, salt and pepper. Cook 30 to 40 minutes or until greens are done.

SMOTHERED CHICKEN

INGREDIENTS:
 1/3 cup all-purpose flour
 ¼ tsp. paprika
 Salt and pepper to taste
 2 ½ to 3-pound broiler-fryer chicken
 ¼-cup vegetable oil
 1 ½ cup water
 1 small onion

DIRECTIONS: Combine flour, salt, pepper and paprika. Coat chicken with flour mixture. Heat oil in large heavy skillet. Brown chicken on all sides; remove from skillet. Brown remaining flour mixture in oil until golden brown, stirring constantly. Slowly stir in water. Return chicken to skillet; add onion. Cover and cook over low heat until done, about 25 to 30 minutes.

Turkey Soufflé

INGREDIENTS:

    1 tablespoon of butter
    7 slices of wheat bread (remove crust and cut in cubes)
    ½-pound fresh mushrooms or 2-4 ounce cans
    3 tablespoons of butter
    3 cups diced cooked turkey or chicken
    1//2 cup of mayonnaise
    1 teaspoon of dried green onion
    ¾ teaspoon of salt
    ¼ teaspoon of white pepper
    ¼ teaspoon grated lemon rind
    1-8 ounce can water chestnuts, sliced and drained
    1-2 ounce jar pimentos, drained and chopped
    3 large eggs, beaten until very light
    1 ½ cup of milk
    ½-10 ½ ounce can of cream of celery soup, undiluted
    1 can of mushroom soup
    1 cup shredded sharp cheese

DIRECTIONS: Preheat oven to 325 degrees. Grease baking dish with 1 tablespoon of butter, then line dish with bread cubes (save some for later). Sauté mushrooms in the butter for 7 to 10 minutes. Drain on paper towel and slice. In a large bowl combine turkey, mayonnaise, onion, salt, pepper, lemon rind, and spread evenly over the bread cubes. Place a layer of half water chestnuts over this and layer of pimentos and layer of mushrooms and another layer of water chestnuts. Sprinkle the remaining bread cubes over the mixture. Add beaten eggs to milk and pour over entire dish. Cover and chill for several hours or overnight. Before placing in oven, combine celery and mushroom soup over top and sprinkle with paprika. Bake for 1 hour or until the soufflé sets. Sprinkle shredded cheese over the dish the last 10 minutes of cooking. Test with silver knife for doneness and if done the knife should come out clean. Hold in over for 30 minutes before serving.

FRIED OKRA

INGREDIENTS:
- 1 ½ pound of fresh okra
- 1 egg white
- 2 teaspoons of freshly ground black pepper
- 1 teaspoon of chili powder
- ½ cup of cornmeal
- Nonstick cooking spray

DIRECTIONS: Wash and dry the okra (if there are any steams on the okra, cut them off). In a large bowl, beat egg white well and mix in the black pepper and chili powder. Toss the okra in the egg white mixture, coating each piece well. Remove the okra and roll in the cornmeal. Spray some cooking spray in a hot cast iron skillet. Place the okra in the skillet and cook on each side for 5 to 7 minutes (or until it turns brown). Makes about 15-20 pieces.

VEGETABLE LASAGNA

INGREDIENTS:

    1 8-ounce package lasagna noodles

    3 carrots, cut into ¼-inch think slices

    1-cup chopped broccoli

    1 cup of ¼ inch thick slices zucchini

    1 cup of ¼ inch thick slices crookneck squash

    2 10-ounces packages frozen chopped spinach, thawed

    1 8-ounce container ricotta cheese

    1 26-ounce jar tomato sauce with Mushrooms

    12 ounces mozzarella cheese, shredded

    ½ cup grated Parmesan cheese

DIRECTIONS: Bring 3 quarts water to a boil in a 6-quart pot over high heat. Add lasagna noodle and cook 5 minutes. Add carrots; cook 2 more minutes. Add broccoli, zucchini, and crooked neck squash and cook the final 2 minutes or until pasta is tender. Drain well. Squeeze the liquid out of the spinach. Mix spinach with ricotta cheese. Preheat oven to 400 degrees in 13"x9" baking pan, spread 1/3 of the tomato sauce, and arrange half of noodles on sauce. Put half of each of the vegetables, spinach mixture, and mozzarella cheese on the noodles. Pour half of the remaining tomato sauce over these layers. Repeat layering and top with remaining sauce. Sprinkle with parmesan cheese,place on a large baking sheet that has been lined with foil. Bake lasagna, uncovered, about 30 minutes or until hot in the center. Let stand 10 minutes before serving. (Lasagna may be assembled up to 2 days before baking and refrigerated, covered, until one hour before baking. If cold, bake for one hour at 350 degrees. Serve with Italian bread or rolls, a green salad with dressing. Yield 8 servings.

FANCY POTATOES

INGREDIENTS:

    5 lbs. potatoes (peeled and cut into chunks)
    1 stick of butter
    3 Chicken breasts (cut into cubes)
    1 chopped onion
    1 cup water
    Seasonings

DIRECTIONS: Place raw potatoes, butter, chicken breast, onion and water in a rice cooker. Season well. Turn on rice cooker on, when the bell rings, it's done. Serve over rice, with bread or as a side dish. You may substitute the chicken with shrimp or any meat. If you use this as a side dish, all you need is one chicken breast. However if you want this to be your main meal, you will want to add more meat.

POTATO PANCAKES

INGREDIENTS:
   4 cups grated raw potatoes
   3 tbsp. grated onion
   1 tsp. salt
   2 eggs
   ¼ cup flour
   ½ teaspoon of black pepper
   Canola oil for frying

DIRECTIONS: Mix all the ingredients together, drop by tablespoons onto hot, lightly oiled skillet. Brown on both sides of potato pancake. Serve hot with apple sauce or sour cream.

CORN PUDDING

INGREDIENTS:

    3 eggs, separate
    2/3 cup of milk
    1 ½ tsp. salt
    1/8 tsp. pepper
    1 ½ tsp. sugar
    1 ½ tbsp. flour
    2 tbsp. chopped pimento
    1 can whole kernel corn, drained

DIRECTIONS: Beat egg yolks until thick and lemon colored. Add milk, seasonings, sugar and flour. Mix well. Blend in green pepper, pimento and drained corn. Beat egg whites until stiff; fold into corn mixture. Pour into a 2-quart casserole dish. Bake at 325 degrees for about 1 hour. Serve immediately. Makes 6 servings.

CHICKEN A LA KING

INGREDIENTS:

4 tbsp. butter
4 tbsp. flour
1 cup of milk
1 cup of chicken broth
1 tsp. salt
¼ tsp. pepper
1 can sliced mushrooms (optional)
1 green pepper, chopped
2 tbsp. butter
1 pimento
2 cups cooked chicken, cut in 1-inch cubes
2 egg yolks, beaten slightly
¼-cup chicken broth

DIRECTIONS: Make a white sauce of the first six ingredients. Sauté mushrooms and green peppers in butter about 10 minutes, stirring frequently to prevent over browning; add to white sauce along with the pimento and chicken and continue heating until chicken is thoroughly hot. Just before serving, add the beaten egg yolks mixed with ¼-cup chicken broth, very slowly, stirring continually. Serve on hot noodle ring.

Organic Herbed Cream Cheese Dip

INGREDIENTS:

    4oz. organic sour cream (or non-dairy substitute)
    16oz. organic cream cheese (or non-dairy substitute)
    ¼ cup fresh, organic oregano, chopped
    ¼ cup fresh organic basil, chopped
    ¼ cup fresh organic rosemary, chopped
    2 cloves organic garlic, minced
    Sea salt and fresh cracked black pepper to taste
    3lbs. favorite dipping vegetables

INSTRUCTIONS: In a large bowl, mix sour cream, cream cheese, herbs and salt and pepper. Refrigerate over night. Remix before serving with fresh vegetables.

TUNA QUESADILLAS

INGREDIENTS:

    1 can (12oz) tuna in water, drained and flaked
    ¼ cup mayonnaise
    ¼ cup prepared salsa
    6 (8 inch) flour tortillas
    ¾ cup (3 oz) cheddar cheese
    Mazola non stick cooking spray
    Shredded lettuce

DIRECTIONS: In a small bowl combine tuna, mayonnaise and salsa. Spread three tortillas with tuna mixture; top with cheese and cover with remaining tortillas. Spray medium skillet with cooking spray; cook one quesadilla at a time until lightly browned crisp, turning once. Cut into triangles. If desired, serve with lettuce.

Spaghetti and Meatballs

INGREDIENTS:
- 1 large spaghetti squash
- ½ pound spicy Italian turkey sausage links (or substitute with ground turkey with seasonings)
- 2 tablespoons olive oil
- 3 cups diced plum tomatoes
- ¼ cup kalamata olives, pitted and chopped
- 1-tablespoon capers, drained
- 3 cloves garlic, crushed
- ½ cup fresh basil leaves, sliced
- 1/3 cup grated parmesan cheese

DIRECTIONS: Preheat oven to 350 degrees. Slice the spaghetti squash in half and place cut side down on a baking sheet. Bake for 30 minutes or until tender when pierced with a knife.

Meanwhile, remove turkey sausage from casings and form small meatballs about the size of a quarter. Heat a heavy non-stick pan over medium high heat and add olive oil. When the oil is hot, add turkey meatballs and cook until browned on all sides. Add tomatoes, olives, capers, and garlic and simmer for 15 minutes. In the last minute of cooking, add basil. While sauce is simmering, scrape out the inside of the squash with a fork into a large bowl; set aside. Toss sauce, squash together, and top with Parmesan.

Serve immediately.

Cabbage Casserole

INGREDIENTS:

4-5 cups shredded cabbage

½ -1 cup chopped or sliced thin onion

3 cups grated cheddar cheese

4 cups crushed corn flakes

1 stick of melted butter

1 can cream of mushroom soup

1 can cream of celery soup

1 cup milk

½ cup mayonnaise

DIRECTIONS: Mix together the 4 cups crushed corn flakes and 1 stick of melted butter in one bowl. Mix 1 can cream of mushroom soup, 1 can cream of celery soup, 1 cup of milk, and ½ cup mayonnaise in another bowl. Layer part of the corn flake mixture, cabbage, and onions twice in a 9x13 pan. Pour soup mixture evenly over all. Top with corn flakes mixture and cheese. Bake at 350 degrees for 50 minutes to 1 hour.

CHICKEN AND RICE CASSEROLE

INGREDIENTS:

    1 cup chopped fresh mushrooms
    ½ cup chopped onion
    1 pound boneless chicken breasts, cooked and cut into ½ inch pieces
    2 garlic cloves, minced
    1 (10- ¾ ounce) can cream of mushroom soup
    3 cups cooked rice (1cup uncooked)
    1 cup of green peppers and yellow peppers
    ¼-teaspoon ground black pepper
    1 bag of shredded sharp cheddar cheese (8oz.)
    Vegetable cooking spray

DIRECTIONS: Add chopped mushrooms. Cook and stir over high heat about 2 minutes. Add onion and chicken breast pieces. Reduce heat to medium high and cook until chicken is just cooked through, stirring in garlic the last minute or so. Add undiluted mushroom soup. Remove pan from heat. Stir in the cooked rice, and pepper. Spoon mixture into a 2-quart baking dish sprayed with a non-stick product. Bake at 400 degrees, uncovered, for 15-20 minutes. Remove from oven. Top with Cheddar cheese and breadcrumbs (a bit of grated parmesan mixed in with the crumbs is optional). Return to oven until cheese melts.

BAKED MULLETS

INGREDIENTS:

1 tomato

1 or ½ onion it depends on how much fish you are going to prepare.

½ teaspoon of lemon juice.

DIRECTIONS: Let fish get half-done, then you slice the tomato and onion on top of the fish, and cover with aluminum foil. Bake for 25-30minutes on 350 degrees.

Gazpacho

INGREDIENTS:

- 1 cup of chopped tomatoes
- ½-cup green pepper (chopped)
- ½-cup celery (chopped)
- ½ cup of cucumber (chopped)
- ¼-cup green onion (chopped)
- 1 tablespoon of olive oil
- 2-teaspoon parsley (chopped)
- 1 small garlic clove (chopped)
- 1 teaspoon of salt
- ¼ teaspoon of black pepper
- 2 cups of tomato juice
- ½ teaspoon of soy sauce

DIRECTIONS: Mix and let set over night, eat over whatever you like or eat as cold soup.

Turkey Lasagna

INGREDIENTS:

    2 packages of ground turkey (32 oz.)
    1 egg
    1-tablespoon olive oil
    1 jar (26 ounce) spaghetti sauce
    1 (15oz.) ricotta cheese
    1 tablespoon parsley flakes
    1 teaspoon of black pepper
    ½ cup of grated parmesan cheese
    6 lasagna noodles, cooked according to package directions
    1 package (8 ounces) shredded Italian cheese blend

DIRECTIONS: Preheat oven to 375 degrees. Heat oil in a large non-stick skillet, over medium high heat. Crumble and cook turkey until no longer pink, about 5 minutes; drain. Stir in spaghetti sauce, black pepper, and parsley flakes, set aside. Combine parmesan cheese, ricotta cheese, and Italian cheese blend. Spoon some spaghetti sauce into the bottom of a 9x13 inch baking pan. Layer on 3 lasagna noodles, half of the spaghetti sauce, and half of the cheese. Repeat with remaining ingredients. Bake until hot and bubbly, about 30 minutes.

Hummus Wrap

INGREDIENTS:
- 1 tablespoon of fresh parsley, chopped
- Cracked wheat
- 1 tomato, diced
- 1 cucumber, diced
- 1 onions, diced
- 1-teaspoon lemon juice
- 1-teaspoon salt
- 1-teaspoon olive oil
- hummus dip
- 1 or 2 Spinach wrap

DIRECTIONS: Mixed all ingredients in large bowl. Spoon mixed onto spinach wrap, and roll mixture.

LASAGNA

INGREDIENTS:
- 2 1/2 cups grated parmesan cheese
- 4 ounces grated cheddar cheese
- 15 ounces of ricotta cheese
- 8 ounces grated mozzarella cheese
- 1 egg
- 1 teaspoon garlic, minced
- salt and freshly ground pepper
- 1 tablespoon olive oil
- 1 jar (26 ounce) spaghetti sauce
- 8 lasagna noodles, cooked according to package directions
- 1 package (8 ounces) shredded Italian cheese blend

DIRECTIONS: Preheat oven to 375 degrees. Heat oil in a large non-stick skillet, over medium high heat. Crumble and cook turkey until no longer pink, about 5 minutes; drain. Stir in spaghetti sauce. Spoon some spaghetti sauce into the bottom of a 9x13 inch baking pan. Layer on 3 lasagna noodles, half of the spaghetti sauce, and half of the cheese. Repeat with remaining ingredients. Bake until hot and bubbly, about 30 minutes.

BBQ Tofu Patties

INGREDIENTS:

- ½ cup shredded carrots
- ½ cup of bread cubes
- ½ cup of bread crumbs
- 1 package of smoked tofu
- ½ cup of brown rice
- ½ cup of bread cubes
- ½ cup of onions, chopped and diced
- ½ cup of bell peppers, chopped and diced
- ½ cup of mushrooms, chopped and diced
- ½ cup of bread crumbs
- ½ cup of vegetable broth powder
- BBQ sauce

DIRECTIONS: Mixed all the ingredients in a large bowl, form ingredients into patties. Turn on medium heat and place in a non-stick pan over medium heat. Cook until both sides are golden brown.

JERKED CHICKEN

INGREDIENTS:

- 5 pounds chicken pieces
- 2 cups distilled white vinegar, plus 1 teaspoon
- 2 cups finely chopped scallions
- 2 scotch bonnets, seeded and minced (please wear gloves)
- 2 tablespoons soy sauce
- 4 tablespoons fresh lime juice
- 5 teaspoons ground allspice
- 2 bay leaves
- 6 cloves garlic, minced
- 1 tablespoon salt
- 2 teaspoons sugar
- 1 1/2 teaspoons dried thyme, crumbled
- 1 teaspoon cinnamon

DIRECTIONS: Rinse chicken pieces well in 2 cups of the vinegar, drain, transfer to 2 sealable plastic bags and set aside. In the bowl of a food processor combine remaining 1 teaspoon vinegar, scallions, Scotch bonnets, soy sauce, lime juice, allspice, bay leaves, garlic, salt, sugar, thyme, and cinnamon. Rinse chicken pieces well under cold running water and pat dry with paper towels. Divide chicken pieces between 2 gallon plastic sealable bags and divide marinade evenly between the 2. Turn bags over to evenly distribute marinade, and refrigerate chicken for at least 24 hours and up to 2 days. On an oiled grill rack set about 6 inches above red-hot coals, grill chicken (in batches if necessary), covered, for 10 to 15 minutes on each side, or until cooked through. Transfer to a warm platter and keep warm until serving. Serve with fried plantains, rice, or bread.

Chicken Bake

INGREDIENTS:

   6 boneless skinless chicken breast halves, (about 2lbs.)
   2 tablespoons of lemon juice, divided
   ¼ teaspoon of salt
   ¼ teaspoon of black pepper
   1 cup (4oz.) crumbled feta cheese
   ¼ cup of diced red pepper
   ¼ cup of diced fresh parsley

DIRECTIONS: Preheat oven to 350 degrees. Arrange chicken in 13x9-inch baking dish. Drizzle with 1 tablespoon of lemon juice. Season with salt, and black pepper. Top with feta cheese; drizzle with remaining 1 tablespoon of lemon juice. Bake for 35- 40 minutes, or until chicken is cooked through. Sprinkle with red pepper and parsley.

Samosas

INGREDIENTS:

1 1/2 cups all-purpose flour

3/4 teaspoon salt

1 tablespoon ghee, clarified butter or vegetable oil, plus 1/4
cup, plus extra, for frying

6 to 8 tablespoons ice water

1 teaspoon ground coriander seeds

1/2 cup chopped yellow onions

2 teaspoons minced fresh ginger

2 teaspoons minced garlic

2 hot green chilie peppers, minced

1 teaspoon garam masala

1 teaspoon salt

1/2 teaspoon turmeric

1/8 teaspoon cayenne

2 large baking potatoes, (russets), about 1 1/2 pounds,
peeled, cut into 1/2 inch dice, and boiled until just tender

1/2 cup cooked and drained green peas

2 tablespoons chopped fresh cilantro leaves

2 teaspoons fresh lemon juice

DIRECTIONS: To make the dough, sift the flour and salt into medium bowl. Add 1 tablespoon of the clarified butter and rub the mixture between the palms of your hands to evenly distribute, letting the fat-coated flour fall back into the bowl. Continue until the flour is evenly coated. Add 6 tablespoons of the water, mix, and work until the dough comes together. Turn onto a lightly floured surface and knead for 4 minutes into a firm dough. Cover with a kitchen towel and let rest for 30 minutes. To make the filling, in a large saute pan or skillet, heat the remaining 1/4 cup of clarified butter over medium-high heat. Add the coriander seeds and cook, stirring, for 10 seconds. Add the onions and ginger, and cook, stirring, until starting to caramelize, about 5 minutes. Add the garlic, chili peppers, garam masala, salt, turmeric, and cayenne, and cook, stirring, until fragrant, 30 to 45 seconds. Add the potatoes and cook, stirring until the potatoes start to color and become dry, about 3 minutes. Add the peas and cook, stirring, for 1 minute. Remove from the heat and add the cilantro and lemon juice. Stir to combine, and then adjust the seasoning, to taste. Let sit until cool enough to handle.

On a lightly floured surface, knead the dough for 1 minute. Divide into 8 equal portions and roll into smooth balls. Place each ball on the floured surface and roll into a thin circle, about 6-inches in diameter. Cut each circle in half (2semi-circles). Spoon about 2 teaspoons of filling in the center of each semi-circle. Brush the edges with water and fold the dough over the filling. Press the edges together to seal. Place on a baking sheet and repeat with the remaining ingredients.

Preheat the oil in a large pot to 350 degrees. Add the pastries in batches and cook at 300 degrees F, turning, until golden brown, about 10 minutes. Remove with a slotted spoon and drain on paper towels. Serve hot.

SPICY POTATO WEDGES

INGREDIENTS:

    3 medium russet potatoes, unpeeled
    ¼ cup of water
    ¼ cup of melted margarine
    ¼ cup of olive oil
    1 teaspoon of hot pepper sauce
    1 package of any seasoned coating mix
    2 tablespoon of grated Parmesan cheese
    Salt
    Pepper

DIRECTIONS: Cut potatoes length-wise into spears. Mix water and pepper sauce in plate. Combine seasoned coating mix and grated cheese in plastic bag. Dip potato spears in plate and moisten on all sides. Shake in plastic bag to coat well. Remove and place on oiled foil-lined baking sheet. Bake in 425-degree oven for about 30-35 minutes. Sprinkle with salt and serve immediately.

CURRY CHICKEN

INGREDIENTS:

    1 medium onion, chopped

    6 cloves garlic, chopped

    1 jalapeno, chopped

    1 tablespoon garam masala

    ½ teaspoon ground cumin

    2 to 4 cloves

    2 tablespoons olive oil or canola oil

    2 tablespoons curry powder

    1 ¼ cup water

    1 chicken, cut into 8 pieces

    4 medium potatoes, peeled and diced

    Kosher salt

    Steamed white or brown rice, for serving

DIRECTIONS: In a food processor, combine the onion, garlic, jalapeno, garam masala, cumin, and cloves. Process to make a chunky paste. Heat the oil in a large Dutch oven over medium heat. Add the onion mixture, curry powder, and 1/4 cup water. Let fry 4 to 5 minutes. Add chicken pieces, potatoes, and salt to taste. Add water to cover, up to 1 ½ cups of water and 1 ½ cup of chicken broth or vegetable broth, and bring to a boil. Simmer until the chicken and potatoes are cooked through, about 30 minutes. Serve over rice.

BAKED COATED CHICKEN

INGREDIENTS:
- ¾ stick of butter or margarine
- ½ cup chopped onion
- boneless chicken breasts
- 2 cups of crushed corn flakes
- 1-teaspoon pepper
- ¾ cup grated Parmesan Cheese
- 3 beaten eggs

DIRECTIONS: Melt butter in large baking dish in the oven. Add the chopped onions. Remove skin from chicken and cut into individual serving pieces. Wash in cold water and drain on paper towels. In separate bowl mix together corn flakes, salt, pepper, and cheese. Dip chicken in eggs, them coat thoroughly in cheese mixture and place in pan over onions. Bake uncovered for approximately 45 minutes in a 350-degree oven.

CRISPY FRIED CAULIFLOWER

INGREDIENTS:
    1 medium head of cauliflower
    salt and pepper to taste
    2 eggs
    ¼-teaspoon hot sauce
    1 cup of flour
    ½ cup of club soda
    canola oil

DIRECTIONS: Wash cauliflower, and break into flowerets. Cook, covered, in a small amount of boiling salted water about 5 minutes or until crisp-tender; drain. Make up a batter using flour, club soda, salt, pepper, oil, and egg; stir well. In a separate bowl combine eggs, and hot sauce; beat well. Dip each floweret into egg mixture; then dredge in cracker crumbs. Deep fry in hot oil (375degrees) until golden brown.

Garden Squash Casserole

INGREDIENTS:

  3 cups of cooked squash, drained
  1 cup of shredded Colby cheese
  1 can of cream of chicken soup or vegetable soup or cream
  of mushroom soup
  1 large onion, finely chopped
  2 eggs beaten
  2 tablespoon of melted butter
  ½ can of sliced water chestnuts
  seasoned croutons
  desired amount of bread crumbs

DIRECTIONS: Mixed all ingredients, pour into buttered casserole; cover with seasoned croutons and breadcrumbs and drizzle butter over top. Bake uncovered in 350-degree oven for 30 to 40 minutes.

ASPARAGUS CASSEROLE

INGREDIENTS:

    2 large cans asparagus tips or cut asparagus
    ¾ cups of sharp cheese, grated
    1 small can of mushrooms
    1 small package of slice almonds
    Salt, pepper and paprika
    1 ½ tablespoon Worcestershire sauce
    1 ½ cups of cream or evaporated milk
    2 hard-boiled eggs (optional)
    2 tablespoons of butter
    2 tablespoons of flour
    1 large can of artichoke hearts
    crackers

DIRECTIONS: Make sauce with flour, butter and cream, thin with asparagus juice if sauce thickens too much. Add grated cheese and melt, mix well. Add seasonings. Layer alternately with ingredients, top with cracker crumbs dotted with butter. Sprinkle almonds on top. Pour into a dish (9"x13") bake at 350 degrees until hot, about 30 minutes.

ARTICHOKE-SPINACH CASSEROLE

INGREDIENTS AND DIRECTIONS:

Melt ¼ pound of butter and 1-8 ounce package cream cheese in top of double boiler. Fold in 2 packages of steamed and drained, chopped frozen spinach and 1 can artichoke hearts, halved. Pour in casserole dish, sprinkle with parmesan cheese and heat through at 350 degrees for approximately 20 minutes.

Broccoli Casserole

INGREDIENTS:

    3 packages chopped thawed frozen broccoli

    1 ½ cans cream of mushroom soup

    ¾ cup of mushrooms

    ½ cup of blanched, slivered, toasted almonds

    1 large onion, chopped

    1 teaspoon of Accent

    ½ cup of bread crumbs

    1 or 2 teaspoons of salt

    1 ½ rolls Kraft garlic cheese

DIRECTIONS: Sauté onions in butter, add broccoli. Mix other ingredients in casserole dish. Pour in broccoli mixture. Cut up cheese and sprinkle top with bread crumbs. Bake at 300 degrees about 1 hour.

VEGETABLE CASSEROLE

INGREDIENTS:
    1 can green asparagus tips, drained
    1 can of English peas, drained
    3 hard-boiled eggs
    ½ cup of cream of mushroom soup
    grated cheese
    cracker crumbs

DIRECTIONS: Place asparagus and English peas in a baking dish. Slice boiled eggs over this pour mushroom soup. Then cover with cracker crumbs and cheese. Bake just long enough to get hot and melt cheese. Serve hot.

Zucchini Casserole

INGREDIENTS:

2 tablespoons of butter

4 to 5 small zucchini (about 3 cups when sliced)

2 medium onions, sliced

1 can (1 pound) stewed tomatoes.

grated cheese

DIRECTIONS: Sauté the sliced onions in the melted butter until golden. Meanwhile, pare and slice the zucchini. Remove onions from stove, stir in sliced zucchini and stewed tomatoes. Sprinkle grated cheese liberally over top of casserole, completely covering ingredients. Bake, uncovered, in 350-degree oven for 40 minutes. Serves 5 to 6. Can be made ahead, covered and refrigerated.

VEGETABLE CHEESE BAKE

INGREDIENTS:

    2-10 ounce packages frozen broccoli, cooked and drained

    1-10 ½ ounce can of condensed cream of celery soup

    1/3 to ½ cup of milk

    ½ cup of shredded sharp cheddar cheese

    ¼ cup of buttered bread crumbs

DIRECTIONS: Place broccoli in shallow baking dish (10x6x2). Blend soup, milk and cheese. Pour over broccoli. Top with crumbs. Bake in 350-degree oven for 30 minutes, or until bubbling.

HOMEMADE MACARONI AND CHEESE

INGREDIENTS:

    2 cups of elbow macaroni
    ½ cup of grated cheddar cheese
    ½ cup of extra sharp cheddar
    2 tablespoons of parmesan cheese
    ½ cup of Monterrey Jack
    ½ cup of Munster cheese
    2/3 cup of milk
    2 egg whites

DIRECTIONS: Cook the macaroni according to package instructions and drain. Place the macaroni in a large bowl, 1 tablespoon of margarine, cheddar cheeses, Munster, Monterrey, milk, and egg whites. Stir well. Preheat oven to 375 degrees. Place the macaroni in a nonstick casserole pan and sprinkle parmesan cheese on top. Bake about 25 minutes or until the top is browned and firm.

RICE & CHEESE BALLS

INGREDIENTS:

1 ½ cup of rice (before cooking)
1/8 teaspoon of nutmeg
¼ teaspoon of black pepper
4 tablespoons of grated parmesan cheese
2 eggs
¼ lb mozzarella cheese (cut in 14 inch cubes)
Pinch of salt
1 tablespoon of finely chopped parsley
canola oil
1/3 cup of flour
½ cup of fine dry bread crumbs

DIRECTIONS: Cook rice. Stir in nutmeg, pepper, 3 tablespoon of parmesan cheese stir lightly with fork. Cover with plastic wrap and chill well. Beat eggs with fork in pie pan set aside. Combine mozzarella cubes, 1 tablespoon of parmesan, salt, 1 tablespoon beaten eggs (save the rest), and parsley. Heat oil in fryer to 400 degrees. Scoop a heaping tablespoon of rice in palm, add heaping teaspoon of mozzarella mixture to center of rice and cover with another heaping teaspoon of rice. Shape into a ball about 2 inches in diameter. Set each ball on waxed paper as it is shaped. Put flour in shallow dish and bread crumbs in another. Roll each ball in flour, beaten eggs and bread crumbs. Cook in hot oil for 5 minutes. Keep warm in hot oven.

AKAR (BLACK EYED PEA FRITTERS)

INGREDIENTS:
  2 tablespoon of water
  ½ chopped onion
  1 garlic clove, chopped
  ½ teaspoon of onion powder
  1 package of black eyed peas
  ¼ teaspoon of salt
  1 egg
  canola oil

DIRECTIONS: Rinse and drain peas (remove all loosen skins from black eyed peas by placing a handful of peas in the palm of your hands, rubbing them together to loosen skins, discard skins). Place peas, 2 tablespoon of water, egg, ½ chopped onion, 1 garlic clove, ½ teaspoon of onion powder, and teaspoon of salt and pepper into a food processor. Blend to consistency of thick pancake batter, add more water if needed. Heat canola oil, drop spoonfuls of mixture into hot oil, cook until browned on each side. Drain on paper towels. Serve warm.

BREAD CRUMB AND BROCCOLI CASSEROLE

INGREDIENTS:
- 1 package (8oz) of sharp processed American cheese
- 10 oz package of frozen chopped broccoli
- 3- 9oz packages of cream cheese
- 6 medium onions, chopped
- 4-5 slices of whole wheat bread (use blender or food processor to make into bread crumbs)
- 2 cups of flour
- 2 cups of milk
- 2 tablespoon of canola oil

DIRECTIONS: Over medium heat, in a large skillet, sauté onions in 1 tablespoon of oil until translucent minutes. Next, blend milk and flour, pour into skillet. Stir in cheese, blending well until cheeses are melted. Place thawed, drained broccoli into a large bowl, toss with cheese sauce mixture, spoon into an oiled 6 quart casserole dish. Mix bread crumbs with remaining oil. Spread bread crumbs over entire top of broccoli cheese mix. Bake at 400 degrees for approximately 30 minutes.

Fish Stew

INGREDIENTS:

3 lbs of fresh fish fillets or

1 lb of fresh deveined shrimp and 2 lbs of fresh fish fillets

1 can of tomato paste

1 can of water

1 red bell pepper

1 medium tomato

¼ cup of oil

2 garlic cloves

½ (red or yellow) scotch bonnet

1 teaspoon of salt

DIRECTIONS: Combine 1 can of tomato paste, 1 can of water, 1 red bell pepper, tomato, salt, garlic, scotch bonnet, and onion. Blend above ingredients in blender until mixed thoroughly. Set aside. Wash and pat dry fish (or fish and shrimp). Set aside. In a large pot, heat oil. Pour in sauce mixture, cook for 3- 5 minutes over medium heat. Add fish. Cover and cook over medium heat for 20 minutes. If using fish and shrimp combination, add shrimp last 5 – 8 minutes of cooking time. Serve over rice.

Breads

Basic Sweet Dough

Ingredients:
   2 packages of active dry yeast
   ½ cup of warm water
   ¾ cup of milk
   ¼ cup of shortening
   ½ cup of sugar
   1 ½ teaspoon of salt
   5 to 5- ½ cups of flour
   3 eggs

Directions: Sprinkle yeast over water: set aside. In small saucepan heat milk, shortening, sugar and salt until warm; shortening does not need to melt. Pour into large bowl of mixer; beat in 2 cups of flour until well mixed. Add yeast mixture and eggs; beat. Add ½ cup of flour; beat, scraping bowl occasionally. Add enough remaining flour to make soft dough. Turn out onto lightly floured surface. Knead 8 to 10 minutes or until smooth and satiny. (Add flour as needed to prevent sticking.) Place in greased bowl grease top, cover; proceed as for desired recipe variations. Bake at 425 degrees for 20 minutes or until done.

TOMATO CORN MUFFINS

INGREDIENTS:
- 1/3 cup of shortening
- 1/3 cup of sugar
- 1 egg, beaten
- 1 cup of milk
- 1 cup of all-purpose flour
- ½ teaspoon of salt
- 1 tablespoon plus 1-teaspoon baking powder
- 1-cup cornmeal
- ½ cup canned tomatoes, drained and chopped

DIRECTIONS: Cream shortening and sugar. Add egg, milk, and dry ingredients; stir only enough to combine. Fold in tomatoes. Fill greased muffin tins 2/3 full. Bake at 425 degrees for 20 minutes or until done. Yield: 1 dozen.

Indian Bread

INGREDIENTS:
    3 cups all-purpose flour
    1 tablespoon baking powder
    ½ teaspoon salt
    1 ½ cups warm water
    oil for frying

DIRECTIONS: Put flour, baking powder, and salt in a large bowl. Mix well, add warm water and stir until dough begins to ball up. On a lightly floured surface, knead dough. Do not over-work the dough. After working dough, place in a bowl and refrigerate for 1/2 to 1 hour. Heat oil to 350 degrees in a frying pan. Lightly flour surface, pat, and roll out baseball size pieces of dough. Cut hole in middle with a knife (so the dough will fry flat) to ¼ inch, thickness and place in oil and cook until golden brown and flip over and cook opposite side until same golden brown. Dough is done in about 3 minutes depending on oil temperature and thickness of dough. After fried, bread is done top with favorite topping or chile pepper and cheese, then cover with lettuce and tomatoes, onions, and you have a Indian Taco.

CORN BREAD

INGREDIENTS:
- 4 cups of self-rising corn meal
- 4 eggs
- 1 quart of buttermilk
- 1 cup of cooking oil (vegetable or canola)
- ½ cup of sour cream
- ½ cup of sugar

DIRECTIONS: Mix well in large pan. Spray the large pan with non-stick spray. Pour in corn bread mix, and spray top. Bake in a pre-heated oven at 450 degrees until golden brown. Cool and cut into serving size squares. Place left overs in plastic freezer bags. Extra bread may be used for dressing.

MEXICAN CORNBREAD

INGREDIENTS:

    1 (17-ounce) can cream-style corn

    1-cup buttermilk

    ½-cup vegetable oil

    2 eggs, beaten

    1 cup of cornbread mix

    1 (4-ounce) can chopped green chilies, drained

    1 ½ cups (6-ounces) shredded sharp Cheddar cheese, divided

DIRECTIONS: Combine corn, buttermilk, oil, and eggs; mix well. Stir in cornbread mix. Pour half of batter into a greased 9-inch square pan; sprinkle with green chilies and half of cheese. Pour remaining half of batter over top, and sprinkle with remaining cheese. Bake at 350 degree for 45 to 50 minutes or until done. Cut into squares.

SOUR CREAM CORNBREAD

INGREDIENTS:

    1 (8 ½ ounce) can cream-style corn
    1 cup of sour cream
    2 eggs
    ½ cup of vegetable oil
    1-cup self-rising cornmeal
    2 teaspoons baking powder

DIRECTIONS: Combine corn, sour cream, eggs, and oil; beat well. Combine cornmeal and baking powder; stir into corn mixture. Pour into a greased 10-inch iron skillet. Bake at 400 degree for 30 minutes or until done.

Yeast Rolls

INGREDIENTS:

2 eggs
2 tablespoon of sour cream
¼ cup of sugar
1 teaspoon of salt
3 to 4 cups of all-purpose flour
½ cup of warm water with 1 tablespoon of sugar—let yeast rise in water.
1 cup of hot milk
2 sticks of margarine or butter melted (one at a time)

DIRECTIONS: To mix: put eggs, sugar, sour cream, and salt in mixing bowl. Beat well, add hot milk continue mixing, and add yeast mix. Add 2 cups of flour mix well, add 1 stick of melted margarine or butter, add rest of flour (add a little more flour if needed to get dough ready to knead). Oil a large bowl lightly. Place dough in it cover it with a towel let rise until double in size. Turn dough on a floured surface knead about 5 minutes. Then start pinching of dough in biscuit sizes. Melt the other stick of margarine or butter in a small bowl. Form dough like biscuits dip in melted margarine or butter place side by side on large baking sheet. Let rise until double in size. Bake in oven at 450 degrees for about 15 to 20 minutes. Checking often, until golden brown. Oil rolls with remaining melted margarine or butter. This should make about 50-55 biscuit size rolls.

Salads

Dijon Chicken Potato Salad

INGREDIENTS:
   1 pkg. (1 lb, 4oz) potatoes,(diced potatoes with onions)
   2 cups fresh broccoli florets
   1 cup diced cooked skinless chicken
   2 Tbsp. chopped roasted red bell pepper or pimento
   2/3 cup mayonnaise

DIRECTIONS: In large saucepan, bring 6 cups water to boil. Add potatoes with onions; boil 5 minutes. Add broccoli; boil 2 to 3 minutes or until potatoes and broccoli are tender. Drain; rinse with cold water. Place in medium bowl. Stir in chicken and peppers. Combine mayonnaise and mustard. Add to potato mixture; stir gently to coat. Serve immediately or refrigerate to chill.

Hot Chicken Salad

INGREDIENTS:

    2 cups of chopped skinless chicken, cooked
    ½ cup of chopped toasted almonds
    2 teaspoons of grated onion
    1 cup of mayonnaise
    2 cups of diced celery
    ½ teaspoon of salt
    2 teaspoons of lemon juice

DIRECTIONS: Combine and put into baking dish. Sprinkle with ½ cup of grated cheese and 1 cup of crushed potato chips. Bake at 400 degree for 20 minutes.

CAESAR PASTA SALAD

INGREDIENTS:

1 medium head romaine lettuce, cut crosswise into ½-inch wide strip (8 cups loosely packed).
1 lb. boneless, skinless chicken breast, cooked and thinly sliced.
8 oz. (1/2 pkg.) pasta twists, cooked rinsed with cold water and drained freshly ground pepper to taste.
¾ cup creamy Caesar or ranch dressing.

DIRECTIONS: Add lettuce, chicken and twists; toss with dressing to coat. Season to taste with freshly ground pepper. Makes 4-6 servings, Prep. Time: 15 minutes.

ITALIAN PASTA AND BEANS SALAD

INGREDIENTS:

    6 cups (16 oz.) pasta, uncooked
    garlic Vinaigrette (recipe follows)
    2 cups (19oz. can) cannelloni beans, drained
    2 cups (19oz. can) chickpeas, drained
    1 ½ cups (12 oz. jar) roasted red pepper, drained and
    chopped
    1 cup large ripe olives, halved lengthwise
    ½ cup sliced green onion

DIRECTIONS: Cook pasta according to package directions; drain. Rinse with cold water to cool quickly; drain well. Meanwhile, prepare garlic vinaigrette. Stir in cooled pasta and remaining ingredients; season to taste with salt and ground black pepper. Serve immediately or cover and refrigerate. Makes 14 servings (1 cup each). garlic vinaigrette: In large bowl, stir together ¾ cup olive oil, 1/3 cup balsamic or red wine vinegar, ¼ cup chopped fresh parsley, 2 cloves finely chopped garlic and 1 tsp. freshly ground black pepper.

Quinoa Vegetable Salad

INGREDIENTS:
- ½ cup of Quinoa
- ½ cup of corn
- ½ cup of peas
- ½ cup of red onion
- ½ cup of orange/red bell pepper
- 1 teaspoon of sea salt
- 1 teaspoon of black pepper
- 1 teaspoon of olive oil
- 1 teaspoon of lemon juice

DIRECTIONS: Mixed all ingredients in large bowl, refrigerate, serve cold.

Cheese-Stuffed Tomatoes

Ingredients:
    2 pounds of sharp cheese, grated
    grated onion
    chopped olives
    worcestershire sauce
    couple shakes of Tabasco
    Durkee's dressing
    Mayonnaise

Directions: Mix cheese, seasonings, Durkee's and mayonnaise in mixer on low speed. Add chopped olives, peel and split tops of tomatoes and stuff shortly before serving. This mixture also makes good sandwiches.

CRAB-STUFFED TOMATO SALAD

INGREDIENTS:
   4 large tomatoes
   1 (6 ½-ounce) can crabmeat, drained and flaked
   ¾ cup of shredded carrot
   ½ cup peeled, diced cucumber
   1 tablespoon mayonnaise
   ½ teaspoon salt
   Lettuce leaves
   Fresh parsley

DIRECTIONS: Slice off top of each tomato, and scoop out pulp, leaving shells intact. Invert tomatoes to drain. Dice enough tomato pulp to make ½ cup; reserve remaining pulp for use in other recipes. Combine ½-cup tomato pulp, crabmeat, carrot, cucumber, mayonnaise, and salt; stir well. Chill until serving time. Spoon crabmeat mixture into tomato shells; serve on lettuce leaves. Garnish with parsley.

Asparagus Salad

INGREDIENTS:
3 hard-boiled eggs
1 can of green asparagus
1 small jar of stuffed olives
1 cup of mayonnaise
juice of 2 lemons
1 teaspoon of worcestershire

DIRECTIONS: Drain asparagus, heat juice. When cool, add chopped eggs, olives, mashed asparagus and remaining ingredients. This is colorless so mix in a couple drops of green food coloring.

HOMEMADE POTATO SALAD

INGREDIENTS:

    3 cups of white potatoes, peeled, cooked, and cut into 1inch
    cubes
    ½ cup of chopped celery
    ¼ cup of sweet pickle relish
    ¼ cup of sliced scallions (green onions)
    1 tablespoon of balsamic vinegar
    1 tablespoon of finely chopped fresh dill
    1 ½ teaspoons of Dijon mustard
    ½ teaspoon of ground white pepper

DIRECTIONS: In a large bowl, combine all the ingredients, mixing well. Chill in the refrigerator for at least 2 hours, to allow flavors to develop, before serving.

Soups

VEGETARIAN CHILI

INGREDIENTS:

    1 clove of garlic, chopped
    1 package of crumbled tofu
    1 cup of onion, chopped
    1 green pepper, chopped
    1 small can of tomato paste
    1 to 2 tablespoons of chili powder
    1 can of red kidney beans
    Salt to taste

DIRECTIONS: Lightly brown onions, pepper and garlic. Add salt. Add tomato paste and little water if needed. Add kidney beans and chili powder. Cover and cook on low heat for 30 minutes. stirring occasionally. Double the recipe as needed. The sauce can be made up a day or two ahead and then add beans, chili powder, and heat when ready to serve. Packaged chili mix may be used instead of regular chili powder if desired.

Vegetable-Bean Chowder

INGREDIENTS:
Nonstick cooking spray
½ cup chopped onion
½ cup chopped celery
½ cup of red or green pepper
2 cups of water
½ teaspoon salt
2 cups cubed peeled potatoes
1 cup carrot slices
1 can (15 ounces) cream-style corn
1 can (15 ounces) black beans rinsed and drained
¼ teaspoon dried tarragon leaves
¼ teaspoon black pepper
2 cups 1% low-fat milk
2 tablespoons cornstarch

DIRECTIONS: Spray large saucepan with cooking spray; heat over medium heat until hot. Add onion and celery. Cook and stir 3 minutes or until tender. Add water and salt. Bring to a boil over high heat. Add potatoes and carrots. Reduce heat to medium-low. Simmer covered, 10 minutes or until potatoes and carrots are tender. Stir in corn, beans, tarragon and pepper. Simmer, covered, 10 minutes or until heated through. Stir milk into cornstarch in medium bowl until smooth, stir into vegetable mixture. Simmer, uncovered until thickened.

Cajun Gumbo

Ingredients:
- 1 chicken skinned
- 1-2 pounds of ground turkey sausage
- 3 leeks or green onions
- 1 bell pepper
- Salt and pepper to taste

Directions: Cut chicken into pieces and boil for 30 minutes. Add turkey sausage, finely chopped green onion, bell pepper, salt and pepper. Cook for another 30 minutes on rolling boil. Serve hot over rice in a bowl.

Split Pea Soup

Ingredients:
- 1-12 or 16 ounce package of dry split peas
- ½ cup of chopped onion
- ½ teaspoon minced dried garlic
- 1 cup chopped celery with leaves
- ½ cup of chopped carrots
- 1 bay leaf
- 1 clove garlic
- 1 dash of tabasco sauce

Directions: Wash and cover peas with water and soak over night. Combine all ingredients with enough additional water to cover well and cook slowly for about 6 hours. This can be cooked overnight in a slow crock-pot. Pass the soup through a strainer and add salt and pepper to your taste. The soup should have a smooth, thick, and creamy consistency.

Desserts

Mango Parfait

INGREDIENTS:

    3 cups diced mango (about 2 pounds mangoes, peeled and cubed)

    1 to 2 tablespoons honey, or to taste

    ¼ teaspoon vanilla extract

    2 cups whipping cream

DIRECTIONS: In a food processor or blender puree mango, honey, and vanilla until smooth. Assemble using parfait or stemmed glasses spoon a 2-inch-thick layer of mango top with a layer of whipping cream and repeat layering. Chill until ready to serve.

MaryAnn's Banana Dessert

INGREDIENTS:
- 2 cups cool whip
- 2 tablespoons sugar
- 15 cream-filled chocolate sandwich cookies crushed
- 4 bananas, sliced
- ¼ cup chopped pecans, toasted
- chocolate syrup

DIRECTIONS: Fill a large glass bowl or small parfait glasses with half the cookies, banana slices, nuts and half the whipped cream. Drizzle chocolate syrup over the cream, then layer the remaining cookies, bananas, remaining whipped cream, a little more chocolate syrup, and then toasted nuts. Serve.

Baked Alaska

INGREDIENTS:
  1-pound cake
  Ice cream
  Meringue made from whipping egg whites with sugar

DIRECTIONS: Split the cake horizontally into two or three layers. Put your favorite ice cream between the layers and "frost" with the meringue. The cake should be on something that can go in the oven, go to the table, and look nice. At serving time, take Alaska from freezer and put into a preheated 500-degree oven until meringue is to the brownness desired. Watch, because it only takes a few minutes. You will want to serve it immediately. If you want individual baked Alaska, you will follow the same instructions except to cut the cake into small sizes.

Carrot Cake

INGREDIENTS:

    1 ¾ cups of flour unbleached
    ¼ whole wheat flour
    2 cups of grated carrots
    2 teaspoon of baking powder
    ½ teaspoon of salt
    1 teaspoon of cinnamon
    1 ½ cup of canola oil
    1 ½ cups of honey
    4 eggs
    ¾ cups of chopped nuts
    1 teaspoon of vanilla extract
    1 cup of drained crushed pineapples
    ½ cups of chopped walnuts

DIRECTIONS: Grate carrots and set aside. Sift all dry ingredients and nuts together and set aside. Mix oil, honey, and eggs, beating after each addition. Add dry ingredients and mix well, add carrots and pineapples. Grease and prepare 3 cake pans. Bake at 325 degree for about 30 to 35 minutes. Let cool before frosting.

FROSTING:

    1 8oz. package of cream cheese
    ½ stick of butter or margarine
    2 teaspoon of vanilla
    ¾ cup of honey
    Mixed all ingredients well and spread on layers.

SWEET POTATO SOUFFLÉ

INGREDIENTS:

    3 cups of mashed sweet potatoes
    ½ cup of white sugar
    ½ cup of brown sugar
    ½ teaspoon of nutmeg
    2 eggs
    ½ to ¾ stick of margarine
    ½ cup of milk
    1 teaspoon of vanilla

DIRECTIONS: Mixed all together. Pour into greased baking dish. Cover with topping.

TOPPING:

    1 cup of brown sugar
    1/3 cup of flour
    1 cup of chopped nuts
    1/3 stick of margarine

Mix thoroughly and sprinkle on top of soufflé. Bake at 350 degrees for 35 minutes. Serves 10. Can use raisins or coconut in topping.

BANANA-NUT MUFFINS

INGREDIENTS:

    ½ cup of butter or margarine
    1 cup of sugar
    2 eggs
    1-teaspoon soda stirred into buttermilk
    2 cups of flour
    1 cup of chopped pecans
    3 bananas (mashed)
    ¼ cup of buttermilk

DIRECTIONS: Cream butter, add sugar and beat until soft and fluffy. Add eggs and beat well. Add flour, a little at a time, beating each time. Add bananas and nuts. Add buttermilk into the batter stir slowly, mixing well. Pour into muffin tin and bake in slow oven, 300- 350 degrees for 30-45 minutes.

ORGANIC CHOCOLATE CHIP COOKIES

INGREDIENTS:

- ½ cup (1 stick) organic unsalted butter
- ¾ cup organic dark brown sugar
- ¾ cup organic sugar
- 2 large eggs (egg beaters)
- 1 teaspoon pure vanilla extract
- 1 (12-ounce) bag organic chocolate chips, or chunks
- 2 ¼ cups organic unbleached white wheat flour ¾ teaspoon baking soda
- ½ teaspoon fine sea salt

DIRECTIONS: Mix all ingredients in a large bowls, preheat oven to 375 degrees, and spray cookie sheet with non-stick cooking spray. Continue mixing ingredients and make sure there are no lumps in the batter. Then spoon the cookie dough on the cookie sheet. Cook for about 17-25 minutes.

BLUEBERRY MUFFINS

2 cups unbleached flour
1/3 cup of sugar
1 tablespoon of baking powder
½ teaspoon grated lemon peel
1 cup skim milk
¼ cup eggs
1/3 cup margarine, melted
¾ cup fresh or frozen blueberries

DIRECTIONS: In a large bowl, combine flour, sugar, baking powder, and lemon peel; set aside. In a medium bowl, combine milk, egg beaters and melted margarine. Stir into flour mixture just until moistened; gently stir in blueberries. Spoon batter into 12, 2 ½ inch muffin pan cups. Bake at 400 degrees for 15 to 18 minutes or until lightly browned.

PECAN PIE COOKIES

INGREDIENTS:
- ½ cup (1 stick) organic unsalted butter
- ¾ cup honey
- ¾ cup maple syrup
- 2 large eggs (egg beaters)
- 1 teaspoon pure vanilla extract
- 2 ¼ cups organic unbleached wheat flour
- ¾ teaspoon baking soda
- 1 teaspoon fine sea salt
- 1 cup chopped pecans

DIRECTIONS: Mix all ingredients in a large bowls, preheat oven to 375 degrees, and spray cookie sheet with non-stick cooking spray. Continue mixing ingredients and make sure there are no lumps in the batter. Then spoon the cookie dough on the cookie sheet. Cook for about 17-25 minutes.

SWEET POTATO COBBLER

INGREDIENTS:
- ¾ cup to 1 cup sugar or honey
- 4 medium sweet potatoes, cooked slightly
- ½ cup milk
- ½ teaspoon ground nutmeg
- 1 teaspoon of vanilla extract
- 1/8 teaspoon salt
- ¼ cup butter or margarine, melted
- dash of cinnamon
- Use refrigerated pastry dough (enough for 2 layers)

DIRECTIONS: Peel and slice sweet potatoes, place in pot of boiling water, cook for 5 minutes, and drain. In a bowl combine eggs, sugar or honey, milk, extract, salt, cinnamon and nutmeg, stir well. Layer a greased 1 ½ quart casserole dish with half of the sweet potatoes, pour half of the liquid mixture over sweet potatoes, dot with butter and sprinkle half of nutmeg, cover with layer of dough repeat process. Ending with pastry dough as the final layer. Pierce dough several times using a fork. Bake at 350 degrees, 40 minutes.

MARY ANN'S APPLE PIE

INGREDIENTS:

    6 cups pared, sliced apples
    1 cup white or brown sugar
    2 tablespoons flour
    1 teaspoon cinnamon or more
    2 tablespoon butter
    pastry for 2 crusts

DIRECTIONS: Line a deep 9-inch pie with pastry and fill with mixture of apples, sugar, flour, and cinnamon. Dot the apples with butter and adjust the gashed top crust, pressing edges of pastry firmly together. If you roll the upper crust wide enough to allow you to tuck it under the edges of the lower crust at the rim, you can crimp your piecrust into a tightly sealed edge. Sprinkle top of pie with a little cinnamon and sugar and bake it at 425 degrees for about 45 minutes or until apples are tender.

STRAWBERRY PIE

INGREDIENTS:

    2 pints strawberries, rinsed, hulled, and well drained, divided

    ¼ cup each sugar and water

    Dash of salt

    1 ½ tablespoons cornstarch mixed with 2 tablespoons water

    1 baked 9-inch pie shell

    ½ cup cool whip

DIRECTIONS: In small saucepan, place sugar, water and salt. Stir over medium heat until boiling. Stir in cornstarch mixture; boil 1 minute. Place remaining strawberries in large bowl; pour cornstarch mixture over. Toss gently but well to coat berries with glaze. Spoon mixture into pie shell. Chill until glaze is set and berries are chilled, at least 1 hour or overnight. Garnish with whipped cream.

Buttermilk Cake

INGREDIENTS:
- 2 ½ cups of self rising flour
- 1 ½ cups of sugar
- 1 ½ cups of oil (vegetable or canola)
- 1 cup of buttermilk
- 3 eggs

FROSTING:
- 4 oz. cream cheese
- 1 ½ cup brown sugar

DIRECTIONS: Mix all ingredients in large bowl, and place in a cake pan. Bake at 350 degrees for 30 to 45 minutes. Let the cake cool for a few minutes. Frost the cake with cream cheese mixture.

SWEET POTATO PIE

INGREDIENTS:
- 1 uncooked pie shell
- 2 cups mashed sweet potatoes
- ¾ cup of honey
- 1 teaspoon ground nutmeg
- 1 tablespoon of vanilla
- 1 tablespoon of cinnamon
- ½ stick of butter
- 2 eggs

DIRECTIONS: Preheat the oven to 350 degrees. In a mixing bowl, whisk the mashed potatoes, honey, cinnamon, and vanilla together. Whisk in the eggs, one at a time. Pour the filling into the pie shell. Bake for about 45 minutes, or until the pie is set.

PINEAPPLE PIE

INGREDIENTS:

    1 uncooked pie shell (plain pie crust with pineapple slice on bottom)

    1 can pineapple chunks with juice

    1 can of pineapple slice

    ¾ cup honey

    1 tablespoon ground nutmeg

    1 tablespoon vanilla

    1 teaspoon cinnamon

    ½ stick of butter

    2 eggs

    4 packages of instant maple brown sugar oatmeal

DIRECTIONS: Preheat the oven to 375 degrees F. In a mixing bowl, mix the pineapple chunks (and pineapple juice) honey, cinnamon, and vanilla together. Mix in the eggs, one at a time. Then add the 4 packages of maple brown sugar oatmeal. Pour the filling into the pie shell, and top with 3 pineapple slices. Bake for about 45 minutes, or until the pie is set. Yield: 8 servings. Preparation time: 30 minutes.

PECAN PIE

INGREDIENTS:
- 1 unbaked 9-inch pie shell
- 1 cup of chopped pecans
- 2 eggs, beaten
- 1 bottle (12 ounces) of Maple syrup
- 1 teaspoon of vanilla
- Pinch of salt
- ½ cup honey
- ¼ stick butter melted
- 1/8 teaspoon of vinegar

DIRECTIONS: Preheat the oven to 350 degrees. In a mixing bowl, whisk all ingredients together. Pour the filling into pie crust. Bake approximately 45 minutes or until the filling set. Let pie completely cool before slicing. Preparation time: 15 minutes Cook time: 45 minutes.

Sour Cream Cheesecake

INGREDIENTS:

Base:

1 ¾ cups cake flour

1 cup of butter

¾ cup honey

2 eggs

1 tablespoon milk

1 teaspoon vanilla

FILLING:

½ pound of cottage cheese, or use half cottage cheese and half cream cheese

½ cup sour cream

1 teaspoon vanilla

2 eggs

½ cup honey

TOPPING:

1 cup sour cream

2 tablespoons honey

1 teaspoon vanilla

DIRECTIONS: Make the filling before the base, as follows. Beat the cheese until soft and smooth, adding the honey. Beat in the cream and vanilla extract, then the eggs, one at a time. Beat until well blended, then put aside and make the base. Line and grease the inside of a 10-inch loose based layer cake pan or flan pan at least 2 inches deep. Sprinkle a little of the flour on the bottom. Cream together the butter and honey until light and fluffy. Beat in the eggs, one at a time, then stir in the milk and vanilla extract. Beat or stir in the remaining flour, and blend thoroughly. Spread the batter over the bottom and sides of the pan more thickly on the bottom. Spoon in the filling mixture. Bake at 325 degrees for 1 hour. While baking, stir together the ingredients for the topping. When the cheesecake is cooked, spoon the topping over the filling and return to the oven for 5 minutes. Cool in the turned off oven with the door open for 10 minutes only, then finish cooling at room temperature. Refrigerate for at least 4 hours before serving.

BANANA CREAM PIE

INGREDIENTS:

Crust:

1 ¼ cups vanilla wafers crumbs

1 tablespoon sugar

1/3 cup butter or margarine, melted

FILLING:

1 (4 serving size) package vanilla pudding mix, prepared

3 medium bananas, sliced

CRUST: Mix all the ingredients well and press firmly into the bottom and sides of a 9-inch pie plate. Chill 1 hour.

FILLING: Prepare the pudding mix as directed on the package. Place the sliced bananas over the entire bottom of the crust. Pour the pudding over the bananas. Refrigerate for 4 hours or more. When ready to serve, top with whipped cream or whipped topping. Serve chilled.

OLD FASHIONED BROWNIES

INGREDIENTS:

2 eggs
¾ cup honey
1/8 teaspoon of salt
1 teaspoon of vanilla
1/3 cup of butter/margarine, melted
2 squares (1 oz. each) semi sweetened chocolate
¾ cup of all-purpose flour
½ cup of chopped walnuts

DIRECTIONS: Beat eggs lightly with spoon, stir in honey, salt and vanilla. Stir in flour and walnuts; add butter/margarine and chocolate. Do not beat at anytime. Spread mixture into a greased 8-inch square pan. Bake at 325 degrees for about 30 minutes. (Brownies should still be soft) Let cool in pan. Cut into bars.

BANANA BREEZE

INGREDIENTS:

1/3 cup melted butter or margarine

¾ cup of sugar

½ teaspoon cinnamon

1 cup corn flake crumbs

1 package (8 ounces) cream cheese, softened 1 can of sweetened condensed milk (not evaporated)

½ cup of bottled lemon juice (measure accurately)

1 teaspoon of vanilla

5 medium bananas

2 teaspoon bottled of lemon juice

DIRECTIONS: In small pan over low heat stir margarine, sugar and cinnamon until bubbles form. Remove from heat. Mix in the crumbs. Press mixture evenly into 9-inch pie pan to form the crust. Chill. Beat cream cheese until fluffy. Blend in condensed milk, add ½ cup of lemon juice and the vanilla. Stir until thickened. Line the crust with 3 sliced bananas, turn filling into crust and refrigerate for 2 to 3 hours, or until firm. Cut the remaining bananas into thin slices, dipping them in the 2 teaspoon of lemon juice. (Keeps them from turning brown.) Top pie with slices.

COCONUT-CREAM CHEESE POUND CAKE

INGREDIENTS:
- ½ cup of butter or margarine, softened
- ½ cup of shortening
- 1 (8-ounces) package cream cheese, softened
- 3 cups of sugar
- 6 eggs
- 3 cups of all-purpose flour
- ¼ teaspoon of baking soda
- ¼ teaspoon of salt
- 1 (6-ounce) package frozen coconut, thawed
- 1 teaspoon of vanilla extract
- 1 teaspoon coconut flavoring

DIRECTIONS: Cream butter, shortening, and cream cheese; gradually add sugar, beating at medium speed of an electric mixer until light and fluffy. Add eggs, one at a time, beating after each addition. Combine flour, baking soda, and salt; add to creamed mixture, stirring just until blended. Stir in coconut and flavorings. Spoon batter into a greased and floured 10-inch tube pan; bake at 350 degrees for 1 hour and 15 minutes or until a wooden pick inserted in center comes out clean. Cool in pan 10 to 15 minutes; remove from pan, and cool completely.

Chocolate Raisin Clusters

Ingredients:
    1 package (8 squares) Semi-Sweet Chocolate
    1 ½ to 2 cups of Raisin Bran cereal

Directions: Partially melt chocolate over very low heat. Remove from heat. Stir rapidly until entirely melted. Add cereal and mix lightly until completely coated with chocolate. Drop from teaspoon onto wax paper. Chill until chocolate is firm. Makes about 2 dozen.

IMPOSSIBLE PIE

INGREDIENTS:
   4 eggs
   ½ stick of butter or margarine
   1 cup of shredded coconut
   ½ cup of bisquick
   2 cups of milk
   ½ tablespoon of vanilla
   ½ cup sugar

DIRECTIONS: Put all ingredients into blender for 30 seconds at low speed. Pour into ungreased 10-inch pie tin. Bake at 350 degree for 50 minutes.

PEACH DUMPLINGS

INGREDIENTS:

    2 to 2 ½ cups of all purpose flour
    2 teaspoons of baking powder
    ½ teaspoon of salt
    ¾ cup of shortening
    ½ cup of milk
    4 medium peaches, peeled and halved
    2/3 cups sugar
    1/8 teaspoon cinnamon
    1 ½ cups water
    2 tablespoons butter or margarine
    ¼-teaspoon ground cinnamon
    dash of ground nutmeg
    whipping cream

DIRECTIONS: Combine flour, baking powder, and salt; cut in shortening with pastry blender until mixture resembles coarse meal. Gradually add milk, stirring to make a soft dough. Roll dough into a 14 inch square (1/4-inch thickness) on a lightly floured surface; then cut dough into four 7-inch squares. Place 2 peach halves on each square. Sprinkle each with 2 teaspoons of sugar and 1/8 teaspoon of cinnamon. Moisten edges of each dumpling with water; bring corners to center, pinching edges to seal. Place dumplings 1 inch apart in a lightly greased shallow baking pan. Combine remaining ingredients except whipping cream in a medium saucepan; place over low heat, stirring until butter melts and sugar dissolves. Pour syrup over dumplings. Bake at 425 degree for 40 to 45 minutes or until golden brown. Serve with cream or ice cream.

Chocolate Sour Cream Pound Cake

Ingredients:

    1 cup of butter or margarine, softened
    2 cups of sugar
    1 cup firmly packed brown sugar
    6 large eggs
    2 ½ cups of all purpose flour
    ¼ teaspoon of baking soda
    ½ cup cocoa
    1 (8-ounce) carton sour cream
    2 teaspoons of vanilla extract
    Powder sugar (optional)

DIRECTIONS: Beat butter at medium speed with an electric mixer about 2 minutes or until soft and creamy. Gradually add sugars, beating at medium speed 5 to 7 minutes. Add eggs, one at a time, beating just until yellow disappears. Combine flour, baking soda, and cocoa; add to creamed mixture alternately with sour cream, beginning and ending with flour mixture. Mix at lowest speed just until blended after each addition. Stir in vanilla. Spoon batter into a greased and floured 10-inch tube pan. Bake at 325 degrees for 1 hour and 20 minutes or until a wooden pick inserted in center comes out clean. Cool in pan on a wire rack for 10 to 15 minutes; remove from pan, and cool completely on wire rack. Sprinkle with powdered sugar, if desired. Yield: one 10" inch cake.

Baked Blintz

INGREDIENTS:

Dough:

½ pound butter, melted

½ cup sugar

2 eggs

1 cup flour

3 teaspoons baking powder

Pinch of salt

¼ cup milk

1 teaspoon vanilla

FILLING:

2 pounds of cheese or 1 pound of cottage cheese

1 pound cheese

½ cup sugar

2 eggs

Salt to taste

DIRECTIONS: Melt butter in 2-quart casserole. Add this butter to all the other dough ingredients, mixing well. Divide dough in half, putting ½ into bottom of casserole. Mix all the filling together, pour into casserole. Use remaining dough over top of casserole. Bake 1 ½ hours in 300 degree oven or until top is browned. Serves 12 people.

CHOCOLATE CHIP PECAN PIE

INGREDIENTS:
  ½ package of chocolate chips
  unbaked pie shell
  1 stick of butter. Melted
  1-cup honey
  2 eggs
  1 teaspoon vanilla
  1 cup chopped pecans

DIRECTIONS: Sprinkle chocolate chips over bottom of unbaked pie shell. Mix well together the melted butter, honey, eggs, vanilla, and pecans, pour over chips. Bake in 400-degree oven for 10 minutes, turn heat down to 300 degrees and bake additional 25 minutes. Nice and easy.

Sock-It-To-Me-Cake

INGREDIENTS:

Cake:

1 package Moist Deluxe Golden Cake Mix

4 eggs

1 cup sour cream

1/3 cup vegetable or canola oil

¼ cup water

¼ cup sugar

STREUSEL FILLING:

2 tablespoon reserved cake mix

2-tablespoon brown sugar

2 teaspoons ground cinnamon

1 cup finely chopped pecans

GLAZE:

1 cup confectioner's sugar

1 to 2 tablespoon milk

DIRECTIONS: Preheat oven to 375 degrees. Grease and flour 10-inch tube pan. For Streusel filling combine 2-tablespoons dry cake mix, brown sugar and cinnamon in medium bowl. Stir in pecans. Set aside. For cake, combine remaining cake mix, eggs, sour cream, oil, water, and sugar in large bowl. Beat at medium speed with electric mixer for 2 minutes. Pour 2/3 of batter into pan, sprinkle with streusel filling. Bake at 375 degrees for 45 to 55 minutes or until toothpick inserted in center comes out clean, cool in pan 25 minutes. Invert onto serving plate, cool completely. For glaze, combine confectioners' sugar and milk in small bowl, stir until smooth. Drizzle over cake.

FRUIT PIZZA

INGREDIENTS:
  1 package of sugar cookie roll
  1 (8oz.) package of cream cheese
  1 teaspoon vanilla
  ½ cup sugar
  Fresh fruit as needed

SAUCE:
  ¾ cup water
  ¼ cup lemon juice
  3 tablespoon of cornstarch
  1 cup orange juice
  1 cup sugar
  dash of salt

DIRECTIONS: Combine the sauce ingredients in a heavy saucepan. Bring the mixture to a boil. Continue to stir the sauce as it boils for about 1 minute. Allow to cool. Slice dough and roll thin; place in a well-greased 14 to 16-inch pizza pan. Bake at 350 degrees for 10 minutes. Allow to cool. Combine the cream cheese, vanilla and sugar. Spread cream cheese mixture over the cool cookie crust. Slice the fruit and place it on the cream cheese (bananas, strawberries, grapes, kiwi, mandarin oranges, pineapples chunks or any combination of fruits.) Pour the cooled orange/lemon sauce over the fruit.

MILLION DOLLAR POUND CAKE

INGREDIENTS:
   3 cup sugar
   1 stick butter, softened
   6 eggs
   4 cups plain flour
   ¾ cup milk
   1 teaspoon almond extract
   1 teaspoon vanilla extract

DIRECTIONS: Cream sugar and butter until light, then add eggs one at a time. Add flour, almond extract, vanilla extract, and milk, stir in flour. Bake in 10" tube pan at 300 degrees for 1 hour and 40 minutes.

MILKY WAY CAKE

INGREDIENTS:
- 2 ½ cups of plain flour
- 2 cups sugar
- 4 eggs
- 8 Milky Way bars (Twix or Hershey candy bar)
- ½ teaspoon salt
- 1 teaspoon baking soda
- 1 tablespoon of vanilla
- 1 cup buttermilk
- 1 cup roasted chopped peanuts

DIRECTIONS: Melt candy bars, mix with sugar, flour, eggs, salt, baking soda, and buttermilk. Mix well. Pour into 3 eight-inch cake pans at 350-degree oven for 30-35 minutes.

Coconut Pie

INGREDIENTS:

    4 eggs
    2 cups of sugar
    ½ stick of butter
    1-7 ounces package of coconut
    1 teaspoon vanilla
    2 cups milk
    ½ cup flour

DIRECTIONS: Scald milk in top of double boiler. Mix one cup of sugar with flour. Gradually pour hot milk into mixture, stirring constantly. Return to double boiler, stir until thickened. Cover and cook for 5 minutes. Beat egg yolks slightly, adding remaining sugar. Gradually add hot mixture to egg and sugar. Return to double boiler, stirring until thick. Add butter, vanilla and coconut. Let cool. Pour into 10 inch baked pastry shell. Top with meringue and bake slowly until brown.

PEACH PIE

INGREDIENTS:
- 1 stick butter
- 1 cup sugar
- 2 tablespoons flour
- 3 eggs yolks
- 1 heaping cup sliced fresh peaches

DIRECTIONS: Mix first four ingredients, then add peaches. Put into uncooked pie shell and bake at 325 degrees for 45 minutes. Top with meringue and brown. Cool before slicing.

LEMON POPPY SEED POUND CAKE

INGREDIENTS:
- 1 cup honey
- 4 egg whites
- 2 tablespoons lemon extract
- 3 cups all-purpose flour
- ¾ cup skim milk
- 1 ½ teaspoons baking powder
- 2 teaspoons lemon zest
- 1 tablespoon poppy seeds

DIRECTIONS: Preheat oven to 350 degrees. Mix honey, poppy seeds, lemon zest, egg whites, and lemon extract. Add flour and milk, mix in the baking powder. Pour the cake batter into a 10 inch tube pan (sprayed with cooking spray) and bake about 1 ½ hours. Remove the cake from the pan and let it cool for about 20 minutes.

Banana Pudding

INGREDIENTS:

   ¾ cup of honey
   2 tablespoons of cornstarch
   2 ½ cups of milk
   2 teaspoons of vanilla extract
   2 cups of vanilla wafers (use more if necessary)
   3-4 bananas, sliced
   3 large egg whites

DIRECTIONS: Preheat over to 400 degrees. Combine honey, cornstarch, milk, and eggs in a medium saucepan. Cook over a low heat, stirring constantly until the mixture thickens to the consistency of pudding. Remove from heat, add the vanilla extract. In a 9 inch or 10 inch casserole dish, spoon ½ of pudding, layer of bananas, layer of vanilla wafers. Repeat, ending with a layer of vanilla wafers. Using an electric mixer, beat the egg whites and 1 tablespoon of honey until stiff, and spread on top of the pudding. Broil the eggs whites until lightly browned(approx.60 seconds). Cool and serve.

BREAD PUDDING

INGREDIENTS:

12 whole wheat bread slices, cut into ½-inch cubes

½ cup milk

¼ cup honey

¼ cup golden raisins

2 egg whites

2 teaspoons vanilla extract

1 teaspoons ground cinnamon

DIRECTIONS: Preheat oven to 375 degrees. Place the bread cubes in a large bowl and soak them in milk. Pour the honey over the bread. In a separate bowl, combine raisins, egg whites, vanilla and cinnamon. Mix thoroughly and pour over the bread cubes. Pour entire mixture into a buttered 1 ½ or 2 quart casserole-baking dish. Place the casserole dish in a larger baking pan. Add water to come up 1 inch of the casserole. Bake about 45 minutes until the pudding is golden brown and firm. It can be served right out the oven or at room temperature.

PEACH COBBLER

INGREDIENTS:
- 1 cup all-purpose flour
- 1 cup skim milk
- 2 egg whites
- ¾ cup honey
- 1 teaspoon cinnamon
- 1 teaspoon nutmeg
- 3 cups fresh peaches, sliced
- margarine

DIRECTIONS: Preheat oven to 375 degrees. Mix the flour, milk, and egg whites together. Pour the honey, nutmeg and cinnamon over the peaches and stir well. Place the peaches in a 9-inch casserole-baking dish, dot with margarine, and pour flour mixture on top of the peaches. Sprinkle some cinnamon on top. Do not stir. Bake about 50 minutes or until the top browns. The cobbler can be served hot or served chilled.

Coconut Banana Pie

INGREDIENTS:
   ½ cup honey
   ½ cup mashed bananas
   3 egg whites, slightly beaten
   ½ cup skim milk
   1 cup shredded fresh coconut
   ½ teaspoon ground cinnamon
   1 9inch reduced fat pie shell

DIRECTIONS: Preheat oven to 350 degrees. Using a mixer, beat the honey and bananas together until slightly fluffy. Using a large spoon, stir in the egg whites, skim milk, coconut, and cinnamon, blending thoroughly. Pour the pie filling into the pie shell, and bake about 1 hour or until firm.

BANANA'S FOSTER

INGREDIENTS:
- 4 ripe bananas, peeled
- 4 tablespoons unsalted butter
- 1 cup packed light brown sugar
- 3/4 teaspoon ground cinnamon
- ¼ cup banana liqueur
- ½ cup dark rum
- 1 pint vanilla Ice Cream

DIRECTIONS: Cut the bananas in half across and then lengthwise. Melt the butter in a large skillet over medium heat. Add the brown sugar, cinnamon, and cook, stirring, until the sugar dissolves, about 2 minutes. Add the bananas and turning, cook on both sides until the bananas start to soften and brown, about 3 minutes. Add the banana liqueur and stir to blend into the caramel sauce. Carefully add the rum and shake the pan back and forth to warm the rum and flame the pan. (On the other hand, remove from the heat, carefully ignite the pan with a match and return to the heat.) Shake the pan back and forth, basting the bananas, until the flame dies. Divide the ice cream among 4 dessert plates. Gently lift the bananas from the pan and place 4 pieces on each scoop of ice cream. Spoon the sauce over the ice cream and bananas, and serve immediately.

MaryAnn's Egg Custard

INGREDIENTS:
- 5 eggs
- ¾ cup of sugar
- 2 cups of milk
- 2 tablespoon melted margarine
- Dash of salt
- Nutmeg or vanilla to taste

DIRECTIONS: Crust for 9" deep-dish pie, mix ingredients together and pour into crust. (Use a blender to mix the ingredients) Bake for 20 minutes at 400 degrees, reduce heat to 325 degree and bake about 25 additional minutes or until pie is set.

OLD FASHION POUND CAKE

INGREDIENTS:
    3 cups all purpose flour
    2 teaspoon baking powder
    8 eggs (separated)
    3 cups sugar
    1 teaspoon nutmeg
    ½-cup margarine or butter (softened)
    1 lemon rind (grated)
    1/8 teaspoon salt
    2 teaspoon lemon extract
    1 teaspoon almond extract

DIRECTIONS: Cream butter and sugar, add egg yokes beat well and add flour. Add nutmeg and lemon rind to mixture, beat egg whites and fold into batter. Use a 12" tube pan and spray with cooking spray. Bake at 325 degrees for 1 hour and 15 minutes.

Baby Food Pound Cake

INGREDIENTS:
- 1 cup vegetable oil
- 2 cups sugar
- 2 cup self-rising flour
- 3 eggs
- 2 small jars baby food (peach, apricot, etc.)
- 1 teaspoon vanilla
- 1 teaspoon cinnamon
- 1 cup chopped nuts

DIRECTIONS: Preheat oven at 350 degrees. In a large bowl, mix the oil, sugar, and eggs one at a time. Sift the cinnamon with flour. Add baby food, flour, vanilla, and nuts. Mix after adding each ingredient. Pour into a tube pan, and bake for 1 hour at 350 degrees.

MaryAnn's Easy Cheese Cake

INGREDIENTS:

Crust:

1 package of yellow cake mix

¼ cup of oil (vegetable or canola)

1 ½ cup of sugar

1 egg

Beat egg, oil, add lemon rinds add cake mix. Mix well then press in the bottom and sides of a 9" spring form pan.

Cake: (preheat oven to 350 degrees)

6 eggs (reserve 2 eggs whites, beat stiff set aside)

3- 8 ounce packages of cream cheese

1- 8 ounce package of Ricotta cheese

1 pint of sour cream

2 lemons

½ cup lemon juice

1 teaspoons vanilla

DIRECTIONS: Preheat oven to 325 degrees.

CAKE: Mix together cake mix (reserve 1 cup of cake mix), oil and 1 egg. Mix with fork, press into 10-inch spring form pan. Add 3 eggs plus the two remaining egg whites (one at a time) mixing well, add sour cream and Ricotta cheese. Continue to beat, add cake mix, vanilla, juice, and rind of lemons, fold in egg whites, then pour over crust and bake at 325 degrees until firm and brown (75 to 80 minutes). May be glazed with any canned pie filling, fresh strawberries, or serve plain.

MaryAnn's Homemade Ice Cream

INGREDIENTS:
- 2 cans of Eagle Brand Milk
- 1 small Vanilla Instant Pudding
- 1-12oz. Cool whip

DIRECTIONS: Mix all well-pour into freezer. Fill with sweet milk to the (fill line in freezer) and freeze. You may use any flavor of instant pudding you like. To make sherbet, instead of filling with milk use orange crush soda or your favorite fruit soda, then freeze.

MaryAnn's Red Velvet Cake

INGREDIENTS:
- 1 box yellow cake mix
- 1 cup self-rising flour
- 1 tablespoon cocoa
- ½ cup sugar
- (Mix the above ingredients well)
- In mixing bowl, add these ingredients:
- 1 stick margarine
- ½ cup cooking oil
- 1 bottle red food coloring
- ½ tablespoon vinegar
- 1 cup buttermilk
- 4 blended eggs

DIRECTIONS: Add all ingredients and mix slowly to blend. Then put mixer on medium speed, beat for 7 minutes. Use 9" layer cake pans sprayed with non-stick cooking spray. For a 3-layer cake use 2 cups of batter in each pan, for a 6- layer cake use 1 cup of batter for each pan. Bake at 350 degrees for 30 minutes.

ICING:
- 2- 8 ounces cream cheese
- 1 large bag powdered sugar
- 1 cup chopped pecans
- Add buttermilk (just enough to keep from being stiff) Spread over cooled cake.

MaryAnn's One bowl German Chocolate Cake

INGREDIENTS:
- 1 box yellow cake mix
- 1 family size (5 ½ ounces) chocolate pudding pie filling
- 1 stick margarine
- 1 cup milk
- 5 large eggs
- 1 teaspoon vanilla flavor

DIRECTIONS: Put all of the above in a mixing bowl, blend on low then turn to medium speed and beat for 7 minutes. Place batter in 9" layer cake pans (makes 3 or 6 layers). Bake for 30 minutes in a 350-degree oven.

ICING:
- 2 cans milk
- 1 ½ cup sugar
- 1 stick margarine
- 3 eggs (blended)
- ¼ cup lemon juice

Mix well, cook over medium heat in a 2 quart saucepan. When mixture thickens, add 1 cup chopped pecans and 2 cups flaked coconut (optional).

Sex in a Bowl

INGREDIENTS:

    1 container of cool whip
    ½ cup of kaluha
    1 chocolate sheet cake
    1 package of Twix, Milky Way, or 3 Musketeers Bars, crushed
    1 large package of chocolate pudding

DIRECTIONS: Bake cake. Let cool and then cut into 1" squares. Place ½ of cake in a large bowl. Pour ¼ cup of Kaluha over the cake, pour ½ pudding, pour ½ candy bars, then ½ of cool whip. Repeat. Refrigerate. Enjoy!!

PINEAPPLE UPSIDE-DOWN CAKE

INGREDIENTS:

1 8 ½ ounce can sliced pineapples
3 tablespoons butter
½ cup brown sugar
4 maraschino cherries, halved
1/3 cup vegetable or canola oil
½ cup sugar
1 egg
1 teaspoon vanilla
1 cup sifted all purpose flour
1 ¼ teaspoons baking powder
¼ teaspoon salt

DIRECTIONS: Drain pineapples reserving juice. Cut pineapple slices in half. Melt butter in 8x8x2 inch pan. Add brown sugar and 1 tablespoon of the reserved pineapple juice. Arrange pineapples in bottom of pan. Place cherry half in center of each slice. Add sugar, egg and vanilla; beat until fluffy. Sift together dry ingredients; add alternately with the ½ cup of pineapple juice, beating after each addition. Spread over pineapple. Bake at 350 degrees for 40 to 45 minutes. Cool for 5 minutes; invert on plate. Serve warm.

CREAM CHEESE POUND CAKE

INGREDIENTS:

    8 ounce package cream cheese, softened
    3 sticks butter
    6 large eggs
    3 cups sugar
    3 cups plain flour
    1 teaspoon vanilla extract
    1 teaspoon almond extract

DIRECTIONS: Mix cream cheese, butter and extract. Then add sugar, mix well. Add eggs on at a time beating after each, add flour one cup at a time, and mix all well. Place in cold oven and bake at 300 degrees for 1 ½ hours.

GOLD CAKE

INGREDIENTS:
- 2 ½ cup sifted self-rising flour
- 1 2/3 cup sugar
- ½ cup vegetable or canola oil
- 1 ¼ cup milk
- 1 ½ teaspoon vanilla
- 5 eggs

DIRECTIONS: Preheat oven to 350 degrees. Grease and lightly flour two 9" round or 8" square baking pans; set aside. Sift flour and sugar into large mixing bowl. Add oil and a little more than half of the milk; beat 2 minutes with electric mixer. Add remaining milk, vanilla, and eggs; beat for 2 minutes. Pour into prepared pans. Bake for 30 minutes, or until toothpick inserted in centers comes out clean. Cool in pans for 10 minutes. Turn onto wire racks to cool completely. Frost with icing of your choice.

MaryAnn's favorite: Old Fashioned Chocolate Fudge

INGREDIENTS:

3 cup sugar
1 cup milk
6 tablespoons cocoa or 2 blocks of semi-sweet chocolate
Pinch of salt
4 tablespoons butter
1 teaspoon vanilla
1 cup chopped pecans

DIRECTIONS: Mix sugar, milk, chocolate, salt and 2 tablespoons of butter thoroughly. Stir constantly until candy come to a boil, then stir no more. Lower heat and cook slowly. When candy reaches 240 degrees on a candy thermometer, cook about 8 to 10 minutes or until a drop of fudge in cold water form a soft ball. Add remaining butter and cool by placing pan in cold water. Beat until creamy (as it creams, the candy will lose its sheen). Add vanilla and nuts and mix well. Pour into buttered 8x8 inch pan. When cool, cut into squares.

Heavenly Hash Cake

INGREDIENTS:

- 1 square unsweetened chocolate
- 1 stick margarine
- 2 eggs
- 1 cup sugar
- 1 cup chopped nuts
- 1 cup flour
- ¼ teaspoon salt
- 1 teaspoon baking powder
- 1 teaspoon vanilla

DIRECTIONS: Melt chocolate and margarine, put into mixing bowl. Add sugar, flour, baking powder, salt, eggs, and vanilla. After this is mixed well, add nuts. Pour into 9x12 inch greased pan. Bake at 325 degrees for 30 minutes. While still hot, cover with a single layer of miniature marshmallows and let marshmallows melt. You may have to put into oven for a brief period of time so that they will soften. You can frost with any type of icing.

CHOCOLATE POUND CAKE

INGREDIENTS:

    2 sticks margarine

    ½ cup shortening

    Cream margarine and shortening

    Add 3 cups sugar, beating after each addition. Add 5 eggs, one at
        a time. Beating well after each egg.

SIFT TOGETHER:

    ½ cup cocoa

    3 cups all purpose flour

    ½ teaspoon baking powder

    ¼ teaspoon salt

DIRECTIONS: Add 1 cup chopped pecans to the sifted flour Mixture, add flour mixture to margarine mixture alternating with 1 cup of sweet milk and 1 teaspoon of vanilla. Grease and flour a 10" tube pan. Bake in preheated oven at 325 degrees for 1 hour and 30-45 minutes.

MaryAnn's Pineapple Cake

INGREDIENTS:
   1 box yellow cake mix
   1 cup self-rising flour
   ½ cup sugar
   (Mix the above ingredients well)
   In mixing bowl, add these ingredients:
   1 stick margarine
   ½ cup cooking oil
   ½ tablespoon vinegar
   1 bottle yellow food coloring
   1 cup buttermilk
   4 blended eggs

DIRECTIONS: Add all ingredients and mix slowly to blend. Then put mixer on medium speed, beat for 7 minutes. Use 9" layer cake pans sprayed with non-stick cooking spray. For a 3-layer cake use 2 cups of batter in each pan, for a 6-layer cake use 1 cup of batter for each pan. Bake at 35 degrees for 30 minutes.

PINEAPPLE FILLING:
   2 packages vanilla pudding
   1 ½ cup sugar
   2- 20 ounce cans crushed pineapples
   2 cups water
   ½ stick butter

DIRECTIONS: Mix pudding and sugar well, and then add crushed pineapples, water, and butter in a heavy saucepan. Cook over medium heat until it thickens. Cool and spread on cake.

MaryAnn's Lemon Tort Cake

INGREDIENTS:
  1 box yellow cake mix
  1 cup self-rising flour
  ½ cup sugar
  (Mix the above ingredients well)
  In mixing bowl, add these ingredients:
  1 stick margarine
  ½ cup cooking oil
  1 bottle yellow food coloring
  ½ tablespoon vinegar
  1 cup buttermilk
  4 blended eggs

DIRECTIONS: Add all ingredients and mix slowly to blend. Then put mixer on medium speed, beat for 7 minutes. Use 9" layer cake pans sprayed with non-stick cooking spray. For a 3-layer cake use 2 cups of batter in each pan, for a 6-layer cake use 1 cup of batter for each pan. Bake at 350 degrees for 30 minutes.

LEMON FILLING:
  3 boxes lemon pudding pie filling
  2 ½ cups sugar
  4 eggs
  1 small can milk
  1- 12 ounce package fresh frozen coconut
  1 ½ stick of margarine
  1 cup lemon juice
  2 cups water

DIRECTIONS: Blend sugar and pudding well. Add water, milk, lemon juice, eggs, milk, coconut and margarine. Cook in heavy saucepan over medium heat until filling thickens and boils (it will bubble). This filling is best when cooked a day ahead and cooled in the refrigerator over night. When cake is being baked, take filling out to become room temperature, ice cake between layers, sides and top.

MaryAnn's Chocolate Fudge Cake

INGREDIENTS:
    1 box yellow cake mix
    1 cup self-rising flour
    1 tablespoon cocoa
    ½ cup sugar
    (Mix the above ingredients well)
    In mixing bowl, add these ingredients:
    1 stick margarine
    ½ cup cooking oil
    ½ tablespoon vinegar
    1 cup buttermilk
    4 blended eggs

DIRECTIONS: Add all ingredients and mix slowly to blend. Then put mixer on medium speed, beat for 7 minutes. Use 9" layer cake pans sprayed with non-stick cooking spray. For a 3-layer cake use 2 cups of batter in each pan, for a 6-layer cake use 1 cup of batter for each pan. Bake at 350 degrees for 30 minutes.

FUDGE ICING

INGREDIENTS:
    2 cups sugar
    ½ cup cocoa
    2/3 cups sweet milk
    1 stick butter

DIRECTIONS: Mix all well and bring to a full boil. Cook for about 10-12 minutes, when dropped in cold water a soft ball should form. Cool and ice cake.

MaryAnn's Caramel Cake

INGREDIENTS:
- 1 box yellow cake mix
- 1 cup self-rising flour
- ½ cup sugar
- (Mix the above ingredients well)
- In mixing bowl, add these ingredients:
- 1 stick margarine
- ½ cup cooking oil
- ½ tablespoon vinegar
- 1 cup buttermilk
- 4 blended eggs

DIRECTIONS: Add all ingredients and mix slowly to blend. Then put mixer on medium speed, beat for 7 minutes. Use 9" layer cake pans sprayed with non-stick cooking spray. For a 3-layer cake use 2 cups of batter in each pan, for a 6-layer cake use 1 cup of batter for each pan. Bake at 350 degrees for 30 minutes.

CARAMEL ICING

INGREDIENTS:
- 4 cups sugar
- 2 sticks butter
- 2 cups buttermilk
- 1 teaspoon vanilla extract

DIRECTIONS: Mix milk, sugar, butter, and vanilla. Then heat, until butter melts while browning sugar, when sugar is light brown add to milk mix. Bring to a rolling boil, cook for 10-12 minutes. Drop some icing in cold water, a soft ball should form. Cool icing by stirring until icing start to thicken. Spread icing over cake.

Banana Walnut Bread

INGREDIENTS:
- ½ cup skim milk
- 2 eggs
- 4 tablespoons margarine, softened
- 7 ¼ teaspoons raw sugar
- 1 cup honey
- 1 teaspoon vanilla
- ½ teaspoon banana extract
- 1 ¼ cup mashed ripe bananas (about 2 large)
- 1 ¾ cups all-purpose flour
- 1 teaspoon baking soda
- 1 teaspoon of ground cinnamon
- ½ teaspoon salt
- ¼ teaspoon baking powder
- 1/3 cup coarsely chopped walnuts

DIRECTIONS: Beat milk, eggs, margarine, sugar, vanilla, honey, and banana extract in large bowl with electric mixer for about 30 seconds; add bananas and beat on high speed for 1 minute. Add combined flour, baking soda, cinnamon, salt, and baking powder, mixing just until blended. Stir in walnuts. Spread mixture evenly in greased 8 ½ x 4 ½ x 2 ½ -inch loaf pan. Bake in preheated 350-degree oven until bread is golden and toothpick inserted in center comes out clean, about 60 minutes. Cool in pan on wire rack for 5 minutes; remove from pan and cool on wire rack. Makes 1 loaf (about 16 slices).

FRIED ICE CREAM

INGREDIENTS:
    1 quart vanilla ice cream
    1 cup crushed frosted cornflakes
    1 cup sweetened coconut flakes, or 1 cup chopped walnuts,
    or 1 cup cookie crumbs
    2 large eggs
    2 tablespoons sugar
    Vegetable oil, for frying
    Hot chocolate sauce, optional
    Whipped cream, optional

DIRECTIONS: With an ice cream scoop, form 4 large balls of ice cream. Place on a waxed paper lined sheet and cover with plastic wrap. Freeze for at least 2 hours. In a bowl, combine the cornflake crumbs with either the coconut, walnuts or cookie crumbs (or any combination). Spread the mixture in a shallow dish. Dip the ice cream balls in the crumb mixture and freeze for 30 minutes. In a bowl, beat the eggs and sugar. Dip the coated ice cream balls into the eggs, then roll in the crumb mixture, coating completely. Freeze for 1 hour. (If necessary, or for a thicker crust, roll again in eggs and crumbs until the balls are completely coated.) Heat the oil in a large pot or fryer to 400 degrees F. One at a time, lower the balls into the oil and fry until golden brown, about 30 seconds to 1 minute. Remove from the oil and place in a dessert bowl. Drizzle with chocolate sauce and whipped cream, as desired. Repeat with the remaining ice cream.

MARY ANN'S SUGAR COOKIES

INGREDIENTS:

- 1 cup confectioners' sugar
- ¾ cup butter
- 1 egg
- 1 teaspoon vanilla extract
- 2 cups all –purpose flour
- 1 teaspoon baking powder
- 1 teaspoon cream tartar

DIRECTIONS: Cream confectioners' sugar, butter and egg. Gradually add vanilla and dry ingredients which have been sifted together. Chill well. Roll out using a floured pastry cloth and rolling pin sleeve. Cut with cookie cutters which have been dipped in flour. Decorate and bake at 350 degrees on foil-lined cookie sheet for about 17-25 minutes.

FRUIT BARS WITH HONEY DATE FILLING

INGREDIENTS FOR CRUST:

- 1 cup of whole wheat flour
- ½ cup of wheat germ
- ½ cup unbleached flour
- 1 teaspoon baking soda
- ¼ teaspoon salt
- 2 ½ cups oats (quick)
- 1 cup honey or to taste
- 1 cup soft shortening
- ½ cup melted butter or margarine

INGREDIENTS FOR HONEY DATE FILLING:

- 1 lb of dates, cut up
- ¾ cup honey
- ¼ cup orange juice
- 1 teaspoon orange rinds
- Pinch of salt

DIRECTIONS FOR HONEY DATE FILLING: Combine honey date filling ingredients in sauce pan. Bring to a boil, turn down heat and boil gently, stirring until thick for 5 minutes. Directions for crust: Combine all ingredients in a bowl and mix well. Pour ½ of crust mixture in a pan, top with date filling. Add remainder of crust mixture on top of date filling. Cook at 350 degrees for 30 minutes.

Sweet Potato-Pecan Pie

INGREDIENTS:

Sweet Potato mixture:

2 cups mashed sweet potatoes

¾ cup honey

1 tablespoon ground nutmeg

1 tablespoon vanilla

1 tablespoon cinnamon

½ stick butter

2 eggs

PECAN MIXTURE:

1 cup chopped pecans

2 eggs beaten

1 bottle (12 ounces) Maple syrup

1 teaspoon vanilla

Pinch of salt

½ cup honey

½ stick butter

1/8 teaspoon vinegar

DIRECTIONS: In one mixing bowl (sweet potato mixture), whisk the mashed potatoes, honey, cinnamon, and vanilla together. Whisk in the eggs, one at a time. In another mixing bowl (pecan mixture), whisk the pecans, eggs, maple syrup, vanilla, honey, butter, and other ingredients together. Pour both mixture in one bowl and mix well. Pour the filling into the pie shell. Bake for about 45 minutes or until the filling sets. Let pie completely cool before slicing.

INDEX